GRACE FOR PURPOSE PRAYERS

Deepen your dialogue with the God of the impossible

GRACE FOR PURPOSE PRAYERS

Deepen your dialogue with the God of the impossible

HOSIAH HOPE

Contents

Time To Seek The Lord.................................9

Allow God To Lead You..............................14

Personal Revival 19

Stand And Believe In Jesus.........................23

Walk With God...28

A Willing Heart 33

God Will Clean You Up 38

Be Committed 44

Seeking God's Presence..............................49

Do Not Be Troubled 53

Surrender To God 56

Invite The Holy Spirit................................61

Raising Your Hands In Battle 65

Hope And Strength 69

Tomorrow Is Not Promised.........................74

No Longer Bound..79

You Are Strong Even When You Are Weak.............84

My Great Defender.....................................89

Freedom In Jesus.......................................94

Strong Faith...98

When Facing Uncertain Times...................102

Secured By God 106

A Peace Beyond Human Understanding 110

No More Fear 113

Divine And Heavenly Protection................117

Put God First..120

God Will Make A Way...............................124

God's Mercy 128
Strong Faith 133
He Still Heals Today 138
The Presence Of God 142
Praise The Lord 147
Godly Passions And Desires 151
Strength From Above 155
God's Covering 159
Give Thanks 164
God Will Order Your Steps 169
Peace Beyond Understanding 173
Prayer For Protection (Psalm 91) 177
The Joy Of The Lord Will Strengthen You 180
Help In The Midst Of Distress 184
A Heart Of Worship 188
God Will Guard You 194
No Time To Waste 199
A Passion For Prayer 204
The Power Of God's Word 209
The Way We Beat The Devil 214
Not Ashamed Of The Gospel 219
Let Go Of Everything Weighing You Down 224
Your Words And Your Heart 229
Knowing Who God Is 234
Set Your Mind On Things Above 240
God Is Good All The Time 245
Remember What God Has Done For You 250
Trust God For The Future 255
Your Time On This Earth 260

Daniel 6:10 (NKJV)

Now when Daniel knew that the writing was signed,
he went home. And in his upper room,
with his windows open toward Jerusalem,
he knelt down on his knees three times that day,
and prayed and gave thanks before his God,
as was his custom since early days.

May this book encourage you daily and assist you in developing a habit of prayer. The Bible tells us that Daniel's custom was to go into his upper room, with his windows open toward Jerusalem, and he would pray and give thanks to God. This was his custom! This is what he practised on a regular basis.

We all need to develop such a habit in our lives. Prayer should be our custom, that's why the Bible calls us to pray without ceasing.

TIME TO SEEK THE LORD

Hosea 10:12 (NKJV)
Sow for yourselves righteousness;
Reap in mercy;
Break up your fallow ground,
For it is time to seek the Lord,
Till He comes and rains righteousness on you.

The bible is very clear with the instruction that this is the time we need to seek the Lord. Now this concept of time is interesting. We all need time, but we can't ever seem to get enough time. We all wish we had more time. More time to do the things we want to, more time to do the things we know we should be doing, but we can never seem to find that time nor can we make more time. The elderly will tell you how quickly time goes by and how short a lifetime is. The young will tell you how much time they have and how long they've got to get things right in their lives. Time is certainly of the essence.

Now the Bible talks about time quite candidly. As we read in Hosea 10:12, the Bible says "...it is time to seek the Lord." Do you take time to seek Jesus Christ earnestly? Do you seek him with an intensity knowing that the Bible says, in Isaiah 55:6 (NKJV), "Seek the

Lord while He may be found, Call upon Him while He is near."

This passage is really a wake-up call to all of us, "Seek the Lord while He may be found." This means there will come a time where it might be too late to seek him, because why else would the Bible tell us to seek him while He may be found? For those people that think such a day could never be, well the Bible says in Proverbs 1:28-29 (NKJV), "28 Then they will call on me, but I will not answer; They will seek me diligently, but they will not find me. 29 Because they hated knowledge and did not choose the fear of the Lord."

Is this not a scary thought? That there could be a day where some will seek God and not find him? This is right here in the Bible, and so we need to take it seriously when the Bible says, "Seek the Lord... while He may be found."

The Bible further talks about time in James 4:14 (NKJV) as it says, "Whereas you do not know what will happen tomorrow. For what is your life? It is even a vapour that appears for a little time and then vanishes away."

Ephesians 5:15-16 (ESV) says, "15 Look carefully then how you walk, not as unwise but as wise, 16 making the best use of the time, because the days are evil."

Romans 13:11 (NKJV) says, "And do this, knowing the time, that now it is high time to awake out of sleep; for now our salvation is nearer than when we first believed."

With these scriptures in mind, can you honestly say that you are living your life knowing that the Bible describes our time on earth as a vapour that appears for a little time and then vanishes away? Can you honestly say that you are making the best use of your time, because you know that the days are evil?

Let us pray for the Lord to give us wisdom when it comes to how we use our time.

PRAYER

Lord Jesus,

Your Word tells me to make the best use of my time because the days are evil. Help me to live with wisdom. Help me to make decisions with a heavenly mindset.

Father, give me a heart and mind that understands the brevity of life in comparison to the joy of eternity. Strengthen me and give me the grace to live a life that is committed to serving Your kingdom.

Your Word in Colossians 3:23-24 (NKJV) says, "23 And whatever you do, do it heartily, as to the Lord and not to men, 24 knowing that from the Lord you will receive the reward of the inheritance; for you serve the Lord Christ."

Father, give me the wisdom to live with the knowledge that everything I do must be for Your glory. Let me not strive to be seen by people. Let me not strive to be recognized for my gifts and talents by people, but Father I pray that I will seek only to please You, to serve You, to be seen by You.

I pray that there will be no love for worldly accolades and trophies in my life, but may my eyes be fixed on heavenly rewards.

Lord Jesus, each day, each passing moment, brings me closer and closer to the day where I will stand before You. Your Word tells me in 2 Corinthians 5:10 (NKJV), "For we must all appear before the judgment seat of Christ, that each one may receive the things done in the body, according to what he has done, whether good or bad."

Father, help me to live with this scripture in mind. Help me to live with the knowledge that there will come a day when I will have to answer for my every deed, for every word I have spoken and for how I used the time that You gave me here on earth. With this perspective, Lord, give me a mind that is fixed on You, King Jesus. Give me a heart that is dedicated to You. Help me to live with an urgency when it comes to seeking Your presence. Holy Spirit, help me to be wise and help me to fight against the distractions of this world. Help me to fight against anything ungodly that seeks to take my time. Let it be my daily practice to seek the face of the Lord and abide in his presence.

Father, I pray that the love of this world may never be found in my heart. I pray that I will never be found outside of Your will Lord, but may I be a believer who is yielded, surrendered and loyal to You. May I be found to be someone who serves You faithfully and wholeheartedly. It's only Your approval that I seek, King Jesus.

Although the days we live in are evil, I pray that Your Word will guide me to invest and sow into things that are above, things that are eternal, and not into the things of this earth which will one day pass away.

Teach me to number my days, Lord, so that I may live wisely.

I thank You for Your mercy, Lord. I thank You for the days and the life that You have given me. May I live this life in a manner that pleases You. May You increase, Lord Jesus, as I decrease; more of You and less of me.

Be glorified now and forevermore.

In the name of Jesus Christ l pray,

Amen.

ALLOW GOD TO LEAD YOU

If I may be honest, for a moment, I have come to the understanding that when I really need God, no one has to tell me to pray. No one has to sit me down and tell me to read my Bible. When I really need God, I somehow find the strength to wake up early to pray. I somehow find the time to open the Word of God despite my busy schedule. I even find the desire to fast and pray, and wait on the Lord until I receive an answer.

However, I have to confess, if I am to be truly objective and honest, my weakness is that once my personal needs are met, the strength I had to wake up early to pray, is no longer there. Prayer becomes a struggle. The time I could find to open the Word of God? That time seems to disappear and I become even busier.

To be brutally honest, my problem or weakness rather, is consistency! I need to be consistent in prayer whether I need something or not. I need to be consistent in meditating on the Word of God whether I need something or not.

Now I would like to pose this question to you. Are you consistent in your walk with Jesus Christ? Do you fight to prioritize Him every single day? Do you remain faithful in prayer? Do you schedule in time to read the Word of God each and every day?

The Bible in Psalm 16:8 (NKJV) says, "I have set the Lord always before me; Because He is at my right hand I shall not be moved."

This verse challenges me, and the key word in this passage of scripture is the word "always." The Psalmist declares that he has always placed God before himself. This says to me that there is a level of consistency. There's a habitual practice and a routine that's followed.

How we should all desire to reach such a level of consistency that we can confidently say, I have set the Lord always before me. I have set the Lord always before me, whether I need something or not. I have set the Lord always before me, whether I am in pain or not. I have set the Lord always before me, whether I am joyful or in affliction.

Let's expand our understanding of Psalm 16:8.

(AMP) I have set the Lord continually before me; Because He is at my right hand, I will not be shaken.

(NIV) I keep my eyes always on the Lord. With him at my right hand, I will not be shaken.

No matter which Bible translation you use, this verse talks about consistency.

I encourage you to pray that Psalm 16:8 will be the anthem that plays in your heart and mind always from today.

Keep your eyes always on Jesus Christ. Set the Lord, Jesus Christ, continually before you. Fight to be consistent within your daily pursuit of the Lord!

PRAYER

Dear Lord Jesus,

You are worthy to be praised and adored. Thank You for Your sacrifice on the cross, Lord. Thank You for dying for my sins and offering me mercy. I did nothing to deserve that kind of love, I did nothing to earn that kind of love, but You still gave yourself for me. All I can do is thank You and open my heart to You so that You can use me in Your kingdom.

Holy Spirit, help me to be consistent. Help me to be consistent in my prayer life. Help me to be consistent when it comes to reading God's Word. Holy Spirit, help me to set my eyes always before the Lord so that if all is well with me, my eyes will remain on Jesus Christ and even when I face difficulties, I pray that you would still keep my eyes on Jesus.

Lord, I praise You, because You are a saviour to those who need to be saved. You are shelter to those who need refuge; a protector to those who need safety.

I worship You, Lord. Your Word in Isaiah 54:10 (NKJV) says, "For the mountains shall depart and the hills be removed, but My kindness shall not depart from you, nor shall My covenant of peace be removed, says the Lord, who has mercy on you."

Give me peace, Lord, even if there is chaos and trouble all around me. Let my heart not be afraid of anything, because You have promised that even if the mountains and hills are removed, Your kindness, Your promise of peace over my life will never be removed. So I will not fear or be shaken, because greater is He who is in me than he who is in the world.

When life appears to be unstable, my soul will not be shaken, my soul will not be moved, because my God is a waymaker. I pray that Your peace and joy would fill my heart, Lord, even if I am facing any obstacles.

Should I come up against any evil opposition, I ask that you will lead me to victory, Lord. Help me to overcome. I pray that You will remove everything that opposes the peace You have given me, the love and power that You have given me.

I welcome You, Holy Spirit, and I pray that You will help me to realize the promises of God. Help me to realize the riches that are in the Lord. I invite You to lead me, Holy Spirit, be with me, move with me, walk with me and speak to me always. I pray that You may be the still small voice that guides me.

Whenever I encounter fear and worry, I pray that You will move to calm my heart. When I encounter things that discourage me, and if my heart is to feel heavy, I pray that the Holy Spirit will be my comfort. Be my comfort in those moments when life hurts, and remind me of God's Word and lead me back into the presence of Jesus.

I find strength in You, Lord, because when I am worn out, when I feel weak, You are a God who renews my strength. I confess that I have joy in my life because Jesus Christ has saved me. I have freedom and a sound mind, because I have laid my burdens before the Lord. I confess that there is peace in my life, because I am washed by the blood of Christ.

I praise You for Your abundant mercy and grace that reigns over my entire life.

I thank You for hearing my prayer.

In the name of Jesus Christ l pray,

Amen.

PERSONAL REVIVAL

Life will throw many things our way. It will throw up things to keep us busy and occupied. Life will send things our way that will keep us distracted and unavailable to really pursue the Lord wholeheartedly. We all have to work. We all have friends and family to see. We all have responsibilities, we have careers and ambitions to fulfil. The list of things we have to do will always be endless. However, the busyness of life can keep us blind to our own spiritual health. The busyness of life can keep us distracted from eternity. When was the last time that you were diligent about fasting and praying? When was the last time you had an intimate worship session that left you revived in your spirit? When was the last time that you spent time alone in the presence of God and came out feeling stronger in your faith? We need to make time for God.

Many people find and draw their strength from different things in this world. As believers in Jesus Christ, we draw our strength from Him.

Isaiah 40:28-31 (NKJV) says:

"28 *Have you not known? Have you not heard? The everlasting God, the Lord, The Creator of the ends of the earth, neither faints nor is weary. His understanding is unsearchable. ²⁹ He gives power to the weak, and to those who have no might He increases strength. ³⁰ Even the youths shall faint and be weary, and the young men shall utterly fall, ³¹ But those who wait on the Lord shall renew their strength; They shall mount up with wings like eagles, they shall run and not be weary, they shall walk and not faint."*

If you desire a revival in your life, then wait upon the Lord. It's the ones who wait on the Lord that will renew their strength! The ones who make time for God will be strong. The people who set aside all of the distractions in this world, and instead, choose to focus on God, those are the people who will be made strong. It's in the Lord that we gain strength, but the choice is ours. We must choose to wait on Him in order to be made strong and experience a revival in our spirit. I encourage you to pray for a heart that is willing to wait on the Lord. Pray for a heart that is patient when it comes to seeking Jesus Christ. Pray for a heart that places God first.

PRAYER

King Jesus,

Thank You for Your goodness and everlasting mercy. Thank You for affording me this opportunity to speak to You. I invite Your holy presence into my life, Lord. Be with me always. Lord, as I call on you with thanksgiving and praise, I ask for Your precious blood to wash away all my sins. May the blood of Jesus make me clean and whole.

Father, I pray for a heart that is willing and a heart that is patient to wait on You, Lord Jesus. Your Word has promised me that if I wait on You, You will renew my strength, so I am seeking strength from You, Lord. I need a touch from You. I need Your strength to see me through all seasons of life. I need divine power from You, to overcome temptation from the devil.

Lord, I pray for a heart that is willing to seek You at all costs. Let me never be too busy to spend time with you. Let it be my heart's delight to seek you. Transform and change my heart, Lord Jesus. Let me be a person who loves the things of the Lord more than anything else on this earth. Give me a hunger for prayer and fasting, so that my spirit will grow. Give me a hunger for worship, so that I can continually offer up my praises to You. Give me a heart that is devoted entirely to You, King Jesus.

Change me from within. That which is broken, mend it, Father. Should there be any voids in my life, fill them with Your love. Today I am asking for a revival within my spirit, just a touch from You, an encounter with You Lord that will rejuvenate me. Holy Spirit, I ask that You will always convict my heart so that I may put God first in each and every way. Lead me Holy Spirit, so that I may always walk in the ways of the Lord.

Lord Jesus, examine my intentions so that they may be good and pure. I pray that in everything I do, I will bring glory to Your name. In all I do, in all of my actions, give me a heart that doesn't seek to be praised but rather may You be glorified. I ask that You keep me vigilant, so that I may always be humble in Your sight. Give me a heart that seeks only to bring glory to you, Master.

Lord Jesus, You alone have the power to transform my heart. You can take a heart filled with sinful desires and cleanse it, so that only pure, Godly desires remain. So Lord, I surrender to You and ask You to perform a special work in me. I bless Your holy name. All honour and all praise belong only to You. Thank You for hearing my prayer.

In the mighty name of Jesus I pray,

Amen.

STAND AND BELIEVE IN JESUS

2 Corinthians 4:8-9 (NKJV)
"We are hard-pressed on every side, yet not crushed;
we are perplexed, but not in despair;
persecuted, but not forsaken;
struck down, but not destroyed."

The bottom line is, regardless of how terrible you think your situation is, God has not forsaken you. You may think that your situation looks disastrous, but God will not allow you to be crushed.

1 John 4:4 (ESV) says, "Little children, you are from God and have overcome them, for he who is in you is greater than he who is in the world."

When you accept Jesus Christ as Your Lord and Saviour, he enters your heart by faith. Now He who is in you, He who is in your heart, Jesus Christ, is powerful and greater than anything that can come against you. Jesus Christ is more powerful than the devil who is in the world.

Now if you really knew this. If you really believed this, if you are convinced that Jesus Christ, your Lord and

Saviour, is greater than he who is in the world, if you believed this, then you would be confident, in every battle. You would be confident even when under attack.

You see, when you believe that He who is in you is greater than he who is in the world, you will not waver in your faith. If you truly believe that He who is in you is greater than he who is in the world, you will call on His name. You will call on the name of Jesus Christ, and He will be your rescue. Victory is certain with Jesus Christ.

The devil may attack. He may scheme against you, but the one thing he cannot do is take away the hope you have in Jesus Christ. He can never take away the faith you have in Jesus Christ. Now, as long as you remain steadfast and strong in faith, you will find that all things really do work together for good to them that love God.

Matthew 21:21 (AMP) says: Jesus replied to them, "I assure you and most solemnly say to you, if you have faith [personal trust and confidence in Me] and do not doubt or allow yourself to be drawn in two directions, you will not only do what was done to the fig tree, but even if you say to this mountain, 'Be taken up and thrown into the sea,' it will happen [if God wills it].

If you have faith in Jesus, if you trust Him, if you have confidence in Him, then you will never be crushed by the enemy. You will never be led to despair by the enemy. The bible has no record of anyone who placed their faith in God and ended up disappointed. We may not know the what, the when or how, but we certainly know victory is certain with Jesus Christ.

PRAYER

Heavenly Father,

Your mercies are new every morning, and Your faithfulness towards me is unmatched. This life may bring with it, its own challenges, its own tests and trials, but I will look to You always, Lord. My faith is in You, Jesus. My hope will be placed in You, and I am so grateful to know that I have an Almighty God who cares for me.

I am grateful that Your Word tells me, in Romans 8:35 (NKJV), "Who shall separate us from the love of Christ? Shall tribulation, or distress, or persecution, or famine, or nakedness, or peril, or sword?"

Nothing can separate me from Your love, Jesus. Nothing I face, nothing that comes against me, can separate me from Your love, King Jesus and I give You thanks.

I declare Romans 8:38-39 (NKJV), [38] For I am persuaded that neither death nor life, nor angels nor principalities nor powers, nor things present nor things to come, [39] nor height nor depth, nor any other created thing, shall be able to separate us from the love of God which is in Christ Jesus our Lord.

Many times, Lord, my natural eyes only see the mountain or the giants of impossibilities all around me, but I pray that You might open my spiritual eyes. Open my spiritual eyes so that I can see the angels that encamp around me. So that I can see the favour and grace that You have placed over my life.

I pray that the Holy Spirit will fill me with boldness and courage. Remind me that I am no longer a slave to fear, but I am a child of God, and I have not been given a spirit of fear but of power, love, and a sound mind.

Help me to realize, Lord Jesus, that a true, righteous way of living is what You describe in Matthew 16:24-25 (ESV), for Your Word says: [24] Then Jesus told his disciples, "If anyone would come after me, let him deny himself and take up his cross and follow me. [25] For whoever would save his life will lose it, but whoever loses his life for my sake will find it."

Lord Jesus, You call us to deny ourselves and set aside selfish interests. You call us to take up our cross, meaning we need to express a willingness to endure whatever may come, for Your sake.

Give me a heart that is committed to following You. Give me a heart and a mind that seeks to exalt Your name always. Give me a spirit of humility, Lord, where I will say more of You and less of me. Give me a spirit that is obedient to You alone Lord Jesus.

Lord, I pray that Your presence will always be with me. May Your presence surround me always.

Watch over my steps, Lord, and while I do not know what is ahead, I pray that You will go before me and give me the grace to conquer whatever comes my way.

I thank You for hearing this prayer.

In the name of Jesus Christ 1 pray,

Amen.

WALK WITH GOD

There is man in the Bible named Enoch. One thing that we're told about this man is that he walked with God.

Genesis 5:22-24 (NKJV) says, "22 After he begot Methuselah, Enoch walked with God three hundred years, and had sons and daughters. 23 So all the days of Enoch were three hundred and sixty-five years. 24 And Enoch walked with God; and he was not, for God took him."

Twice in this short passage we're told the words, "Enoch walked with God."

There is a deeper meaning behind the words 'walked with God.' Consider what another translation for Genesis 5:22-24 (AMP) says, "22 Enoch walked [in habitual fellowship] with God three hundred years after the birth of Methuselah and had other sons and daughters. 23 So all the days of Enoch were three hundred and sixty-five years. 24 And [in reverent fear and obedience] Enoch walked with God; and he was not [found among men], because God took him [away to be home with Him]."

The life of Enoch is summed up by four words: "He walked with God."

The Bible tells us that two cannot walk together unless they agree, so when you think about what we are being told about Enoch, it's a remarkable statement that he is known for walking with God. For two people to walk together they have to be in agreement, and I could even go as far as saying, two cannot walk together unless one leads and one submits. Think of it like this, you will never have two CEOs for a single company or two captains for a single team or two presidents for a single country. Only one can lead. This is the same in our relationship with the Lord. Only He can lead and we are to submit and follow His ways, His commands, and His Word. It is the will of God that should lead us, and if we ever try to impose our own will, then we fall into rebellion, we fall into sin and disagreement with the Lord.

It's important to understand what the Bible really means when it tells us that Enoch walked with God. It means he followed God. It means he was led by God. It means he submitted to God.

Can the same be said about you? Are you walking in habitual fellowship with God? Are you walking in reverent fear and obedience to God?

The Bible says, in Deuteronomy 8:6 (NKJV), "Therefore you shall keep the commandments of the Lord your God, to walk in His ways and to fear Him."

Every believer needs to realize that we live in a world that is spiritually dark. This is why the Bible tells us to "keep the commandments of the Lord." We need to walk in God's ways, because this world will lead you to destruction. In this world, Godly morals are out of the window and sin has become normalized, it's accepted and openly paraded by all to see. Pleasure and selfish gain are the primary motivations that determine a lot of people's actions.

So, as we live in such a world, how can you and I walk with the Lord? How can we walk with Him in habitual fellowship? How can we walk with Him in obedience?

Well, I believe that two cannot walk together if they are going in two different directions. In order for us to truly walk with the Lord, we need to turn our backs on the world and what it has to offer and choose Jesus Christ. We need to reject what is accepted and loved by the world and choose Jesus. I encourage you to turn away from the world and turn to Jesus. Turn away from sin and turn to the Word of God. Make a decision to follow Jesus Christ and walk in obedience to the Lord's commands and His ways.

PRAYER

Dear Lord,

Have mercy on me, Father, and give me the grace to see this world for what it really is. This world will only lead me to destruction, but Your way, Lord Jesus, will lead me to an eternity in Your presence.

Open my eyes King Jesus, so that I can see that there is nothing to be gained from this world. This world will only disappoint me but You, Lord Jesus, will never fail me nor will You let me down.

Lord Jesus, joy, peace, protection, and true contentment can only be found in You, not in this world. This world is filled with fleeting pleasures, and I pray that I will never be drawn to what this world offers. Help me to reject the advances of the world, Lord. I desire to walk with You, Jesus.

Your Word in Romans 13:12-14 (ESV) says, "12 The night is far gone; the day is at hand. So then let us cast off the works of darkness and put on the armor of light. 13 Let us walk properly as in the daytime, not in orgies and drunkenness, not in sexual immorality and sensuality, not in quarreling and jealousy. 14 But put on the Lord Jesus Christ, and make no provision for the flesh, to gratify its desires."

I pray that the fear of God will rule my life. Holy Spirit, help me to conduct myself in accordance to God's Word. Help me to walk honourably and with integrity as a child of God. Father, help me to walk in obedience to Your Word. Help me to walk under the guidance of the Holy Spirit. Let faith be my eyes.

Lord, I desire to walk with You always. I desire to walk in agreement with You. I desire to walk in submission to You. Hear my cry, Lord Jesus, as my heart yearns for Your presence.

I seek to draw closer to You each and every day. May You be my only focus. May Your presence be my heart's desire. Purge me and remove all worldly desires from my life. Remove all ungodly passions.

Your Word in Luke 10:27 (NKJV) says, "So he answered and said, 'You shall love the Lord your God with all your heart, with all your soul, with all your strength, and with all your mind,' and 'your neighbour as yourself.' "

With all that I have, with every breath in me, I declare that Jesus Christ is Lord over my life. My heart is Yours. My soul is Yours. My mind is Yours. I will praise You with all of my strength. I will worship You with all that is within me. I will bless Your holy name forever and ever.

Be with me, Father God. Be with me, Lord Jesus. Be with me, Holy Spirit.

I thank You for hearing my prayer.

In the name of Jesus Christ I pray,

Amen.

A WILLING HEART

God loves a willing heart. He loves a heart that is full of faith, a heart that is committed and focused to seek His Kingdom first, above all else.

David is described as a man after God's own heart, and the book of Psalms talks about the heart extensively.

Consider the following scriptures:

Psalm 19:14 (NKJV), "Let the words of my mouth and the meditation of my heart be acceptable in Your sight, O Lord, my strength and my Redeemer."

Psalm 26:2 (NKJV), "Examine me, O Lord, and prove me; Try my mind and my heart."

Psalm 51:10 (NKJV), "Create in me a clean heart, O God, and renew a steadfast spirit within me."

Psalm 119:10-11 (NKJV), "[10] With my whole heart I have sought You; Oh, let me not wander from Your commandments! [11] Your word I have hidden in my heart, that I might not sin against You."

Your heart is an important area of your life, because the heart is central to all things. When you love, that's related to the heart. When you hate, that's related to the heart. When you are bitter, resentful, or unforgiving... these are all matters of the heart. So, you see, the heart is an important area when it comes to your spiritual health.

It's the heart that the Bible says is deceitful above all things. It's the heart which we have been told to guard with all diligence, because out of the heart spring the issues of life.

Now, if you are to experience true change in your life, if you want real and lasting change in your life, take a look at the state of your heart. If God were to test your heart, what would He find in there?

Proverbs 4:23 (NKJV) says, "Keep your heart with all diligence, For out of it spring the issues of life."

The word diligence means careful and persistent work or effort. So, in other words, the Bible is saying, guard your heart with careful and persistent work or effort.

Being diligent, when it comes to guarding your heart, means that you scrutinize, you analyse and assess the things that you meditate on, and you do this to ensure that those things do not become idols or hindrances in your life. Watching over your heart means that you are careful about what you allow to enter through the gates of your ears and the gates of your eyes.

The Bible says "So then faith comes by hearing, and hearing by the word of God." (Romans 10:17, NKJV)

This says to me that what I hear has a great effect on my heart. We are to guard and watch over our hearts to ensure that the ground is fertile for God's Word to grow and develop our faith. We are to guard and watch over our hearts to ensure that sin has no room to grow and settle.

I encourage you to make a commitment to be the guardian of your heart. Take responsibility when it comes to what you expose to your inner self. Dwell on that which is Godly. Dwell on that which is noble and pure. Dwell on the Word of God, and let Jesus Christ reign as Lord and King in your heart.

PRAYER

Lord Jesus,

I give You my heart. I open up my heart to You, and I ask that You fill me with Your Holy Spirit. Fill my heart with a genuine love that comes only from You, Lord. Fill me with the kind of love that is patient and kind; a love that does not envy or boast.

Lord Jesus, I pray that You will heal my heart from every hurt. Heal my heart from any wounds that have been inflicted by others. Let me not be someone who walks around with resentment in my heart but rather, give me freedom, give me love and joy. May Your precious blood heal every emotional wound and make me whole again.

I pray and declare Your Word in Philippians 4:7 (NKJV), for the Bible says, "and the peace of God, which surpasses all understanding, will guard your hearts and minds through Christ Jesus."

I welcome this divine peace into my heart and mind, Lord Jesus. A peace that surpasses all understanding. Lord Jesus, my prayer is that You will give me a heart that is willing to serve You and only You. Give me a heart that is willing to turn around and forsake the world in exchange for righteousness, for purity, and holiness. Create in me a clean heart, Lord Jesus.

Lord, I pray for a heart that is readily available to obey Your every command, a heart that is fully surrendered and obedient to Your Word. I pray for a heart that has no tolerance for evil or sin. Let my heart be on fire for You, Lord Jesus. Give me a pure and holy passion.

Hear my cry, Lord Jesus, and remove this heart of stone within me. Give me a heart that is sensitive to Your voice and drawn to You and You alone. Do not let my heart be darkened by sin. Do not let my heart be hardened by this world. Father, do not let my heart be troubled by what I see in the flesh.

Instead, I pray that You will overturn my heart. May the Holy Spirit come into my heart and begin to transform me and change me. I pray that You will cleanse my heart, Lord, because on my own I have no power to change. On my own, I have no strength to overcome temptation, but it's only through You, through Your grace and mercy, that I can be victorious.

Lord, I need Your divine strength. I need You, Lord Jesus. I need You to remove everything that does not please You within me. Remove any bitterness. Remove any hurt. Remove all idols.

I declare today that Jesus Christ rules in my life. I yield and surrender, Lord. I give You permission to move as You will. You have permission to overturn my heart and turn everything upside down. Remove the baggage, clear out the garbage and make my heart clean and acceptable to You. Make me a new creature in You, Lord.

In the mighty name of Jesus Christ I pray,

Amen.

GOD WILL CLEAN YOU UP

How can you live a life that is pure and pleasing to the Lord? How do you live a life where you aren't cycling in and out of sin?

These are questions that many Christians, including myself, have wrestled with. Lord, how do I live right? How do I live a life that is free from the clutches sin?

Now, if you've ever made a commitment in your heart that you were going to do your best to live a life that was pure and holy, sooner or later, you'll find out that the pull of sin is greater than your willpower. You and I cannot break the power of sin over our lives through sheer determination and grit. We need Jesus Christ to set us free from sin's hold over our lives.

Consider that Paul the apostle wrote, in Romans 7:15 (NKJV), "For what I am doing, I do not understand. For what I will to do, that I do not practice; but what I hate, that I do."

And then, if you read on further, you'll find that Romans 7:18 (NKJV) says, "For I know that in me (that is, in my flesh) nothing good dwells; for to will is present with me, but how to perform what is good I do not find."

It's interesting that Paul is so honest about his struggle with sin. Think about it, a servant of the Lord, Paul, says that nothing good lives in him. It's also interesting that, although he is mightily used by God, he expresses this conflict with sin and says that he is willing to be good, he is willing to do the right thing, but to perform that which is good, that's where the problem lies.

Now, how many of us can relate to this? How many of us can accept that we know what is expected of us, based on God's Word, but doing it, putting it into action, is a different matter all together. We can all relate to Paul's frustration with himself.

This begs the question, how do we live right before the Lord? How do we overcome this struggle of sin? How do we become clean vessels, ready to serve God's kingdom?

Dear friend, I want you to know that you and I are powerless against sin. You and I aren't capable of cleansing ourselves from the sin in our lives. The only thing you can do is to present yourself to the Lord, as you are. Present yourself to Jesus Christ with a willing heart.

Here's what the Bible says in Ezekiel 36:25-27 (ESV),

²⁵ *"I will sprinkle clean water on you, and you shall be clean from all your uncleannesses, and from all your idols I will cleanse you.*

²⁶ *And I will give you a new heart, and a new spirit I will put within you. And I will remove the heart of stone from your flesh and give you a heart of flesh.*

²⁷ *And I will put my Spirit within you, and cause you to walk in my statutes and be careful to obey my rules.*

I want you to see that, in this passage of scripture, God is saying "I will."

"I will cleanse you."

"I will give a new heart."

"I will put my spirit within you."

"I will remove your heart of stone."

God does all the work when it comes to purifying us. We cannot cleanse ourselves, but the Lord says, "I will cleanse you." We cannot change our wicked hearts, but the Lord says, "I will give you a new heart."

I encourage you to present yourself to Jesus Christ with a willing heart, and He will do the rest.

PRAYER

Lord Jesus,

It is by Your grace and mercy that I am alive today. It's by Your goodness and loving-kindness that I have strength in my body and breath in my lungs. For this, my God, I praise You. I thank You, and I worship You.

Lord Jesus, I ask that You will have mercy on me, Father. Forgive me for all of the wrong I have done. Forgive me, Lord Jesus, for all of the times I have fallen short.

Your Word in Psalm 103:10-12 (ESV) says, "He does not deal with us according to our sins, nor repay us according to our iniquities. For as high as the heavens are above the earth, so great is his steadfast love toward those who fear him; as far as the east is from the west, so far does he remove our transgressions from us."

I bless Your holy name for such love and mercy. I can only thank You, Lord Jesus, because You have not dealt with me according to my sins.

For the sins I committed, I deserved death, but You have forgiven me and offered me redemption and eternal life. For the sins I committed, I deserved to be abandoned, condemned, and cast away, but I praise You, King Jesus, for Your great love. Despite my sins, You have never abandoned me. Despite my sinful actions, You have not turned Your back on me and cast me away. Despite my sins, You have not condemned me, because Your Word in Romans 8:1 (NKJV) says,

"There is therefore now no condemnation to those who are in Christ Jesus, who do not walk according to the flesh, but according to the Spirit."

Great is Your faithfulness, Lord Jesus. Great is Your mercy, because You have not condemned me despite me falling. So great is Your loving-kindness that You have removed my transgressions from me as far as the east is from the west, and so I thank You.

Father, Your Word in Ezekiel 36:27 (NKJV) says, "I will put My Spirit within you and cause you to walk in My statutes, and you will keep My judgments and do them."

Father, I am willing to receive every gift that is from You. I open up my heart at this moment, Lord, and I hold on to Your Word that tells me that You will put Your spirit within me and cause me to walk in Your statutes.

I thank You, Lord, for the cleansing power that is in Your blood. You alone can make me pure. You alone can destroy every evil and filthy habit in my life. Wash me clean with Your blood, King Jesus.

On my own, I am incapable of making myself pure but, by Your grace, by Your mercy, I can be made clean. Remove this heart of stone in me and give me a new heart, a heart that seeks to honour You and a heart that lives only to serve You, Father.

I bless Your holy name for listening to my prayer.

In the mighty and precious name of Jesus Christ I pray,

Amen.

BE COMMITTED

If you are to search for the definition of the word "commitment", you'll find that the Merriam-Webster dictionary defines it as: "An agreement or pledge to do something in the future" or "The state or an instance of being obligated or emotionally impelled."

I want you to pay attention to some of the words associated to the meaning of the word "commitment."

A commitment is a pledge. A commitment is an instance of being obligated. A commitment is a promise.

The Bible calls for us to be committed to Jesus Christ. 1 Kings 8:61 (NIV) says, "And may your hearts be fully committed to the Lord our God, to live by his decrees and obey his commands, as at this time."

Take a moment to really decipher what this verse is telling us. Your heart should be fully committed to Jesus Christ. Your heart should be obligated, compelled, to follow Jesus Christ. Your heart should be wholly devoted and completely loyal to the Lord.

Psalm 37:5 (NKJV) says, "Commit your way to the Lord, Trust also in Him, and He shall bring it to pass."

Have you committed your way to the Lord?

I want to encourage you to make a decision today. A decision to commit your ways to Jesus Christ. Be someone who is loyal, never to be found with a wandering eye. Don't be found giving anything less than your all to the Lord. Make a commitment to Jesus Christ. Make a commitment that you will take action regarding the things of the Lord. Take action today! Don't wait until tomorrow. Don't wait for someone to lay hands on you. Take action concerning your relationship with Jesus Christ today and make a commitment.

As for me, I have decided that I will trust, I will praise, I will pray, and I will worship Jesus Christ today! I will give my all, I will hold nothing back, and I will be loyal and wholly devoted to Jesus Christ. I'm not waiting for a convention, I'm not waiting for the blessing or the miracle; I am committing to the Lord today! Tomorrow is not promised. Today, while I still have breath in my lungs and strength in my bones, I will put my trust in Jesus. I will commit my ways to Him. As long as I am living, as long as I have a voice, I will declare that Jesus Christ is my Lord and Saviour.

Today, I boldly declare that I will! I will. I will put my faith only in Jesus Christ! No one else can rescue me. No one else can help me but Jesus. So I will call on the name of Jesus Christ today. I will call on His name tomorrow and every day after that! Whether I'm on the mountaintop or I am deep in the valley, I will call on Jesus Christ. He is always faithful.

PRAYER

Lord Jesus,

Your Word in Proverbs 16:3 (NIV) says, "Commit to the Lord whatever you do, and he will establish your plans."

Father, in obedience to Your Word, I commit all to You. The plans I have made are in Your hands, Father. The goals I have and all of the things that I want to achieve, I commit them into Your hands.

Lord, I commit my ways to You. I commit my life to You, Lord Jesus. My family, my children, my marriage, my business, I commit everything to You, mighty God. Take control and have Your way. Let Your will be done in my life. May the Holy Spirit lead and move within my heart and in my home so that I can be led to do that which is pleasing in Your sight.

Father, in committing all that I have to You, I am saying that I submit my life to You, Lord Jesus. I trust You, Lord. I believe in You and I believe Your Word.

Lord Jesus, as I commit everything to You, as I declare my loyalty and devotion to You, I also submit my thought life into Your hands. I submit my heart's desires to You. Reshape my thinking, Lord. Let my thinking be aligned to the Word of God. Let my heart's desires be pure in Your sight. This world may try and get me to conform to its ways, however, I pray that You will give me the strength to overcome the temptations of the world.

Friends may try to entice me so that I can conform to their sinful ways, however, I pray that You will give me the strength to overcome the temptations of this world. May I be so committed to following You my Lord, that nothing in this world will take my focus or draw my affection. I pray that my eyes would always be fixed on You.

I pray and I declare Psalm 16:8-9 (NKJV), "I have set the Lord always before me; Because He is at my right hand I shall not be moved. Therefore my heart is glad, and my glory rejoices; My flesh also will rest in hope."

With You before me, Lord, I will not be moved by any situation. My heart is filled with gladness and joy because I am under Your care, Lord Jesus.

Lord, I may not know what tomorrow has in store for me, but I do have faith that whatever the enemy means for evil, You will turn it around for my good. I may not know what tomorrow has in store for me but I do have faith in You as my provider. I trust that You will be my safe place.

Be glorified, Lord Jesus. I am at peace, because I know who my God is. I am at peace, because I know that You are my source. I am at peace because I know You are my protector.

Lord, You have my focus. You have my attention. I look to You and You alone for direction, for strength, and for comfort.

I praise You in advance, Lord Jesus, for all that You have done, all that You are doing, and that which You are still yet to do.

I thank You for Your grace and mercy. Thank You for hearing my prayer.

In the name of Jesus Christ l pray,

Amen.

SEEKING GOD'S PRESENCE

Revelation 22:12 (AMP)
"Behold, I (Jesus) am coming quickly,
and My reward is with Me,
to give to each one according to the
merit of his deeds (earthly works, faithfulness)."

There should be urgency in our lives when it comes to seeking the Lord. The Bible tells us that Jesus Christ is coming back quickly, so we need to closely inspect our lives and assess what we are chasing on a day-to-day basis. Who or what are we seeking each day? Are we seeking a relationship with Him? Are we seeking to know Jesus Christ on a personal, deeper level?

Isaiah 55:6-7 (NKJV) encourages us to, "⁶ Seek the Lord while He may be found, call upon Him while He is near. ⁷ Let the wicked forsake his way, and the unrighteous man his thoughts; Let him return to the Lord, and He will have mercy on him; and to our God, for He will abundantly pardon." Time is fleeting. Life is short, and tomorrow is not promised. The Bible urges us to "Seek the Lord while He may be found." The emphasis is on the condition "while He may be found." There is a timestamp to that statement indicating that there may well come a time when you will seek the Lord and won't find Him because it will be too late. What is clear is that we, as believers, have no time to be one foot in and one foot out. We need to be all in for God. This is not the time to entertain or tolerate sinful habits or behaviours. We have no time for a half-hearted prayer life. We need to always be about our Father's business.

Once again Revelation 22:12 (AMP) says, "Behold, I (Jesus) am coming quickly, and my reward is with me, to give to each one according to the merit of his deeds (earthly works, faithfulness)." What will your reward be when the Lord returns? Have you been faithful in honouring and obeying His Word? Have you been a diligent servant working in the Kingdom of God and in the body of Christ? Exercise what God's Word says in Matthew 6:33 (NKJV), "But seek first the kingdom of God and His righteousness, and all these things shall be added to you."

PRAYER

Heavenly Father,

You are a God who is faithful to deliver. You have the final say over my life, Lord. Help me to set my affections on things above, not on the things of this world. Help me to seek and to strive after You, to chase after heavenly things and eternal rewards rather than the perishable treasures of this world. Give me a desire, King Jesus, to pray like You did while on this earth. Give me a desire to pray consistently, a desire to immerse myself in Your Word.

Your Word in 1 Chronicles 16:11 (ESV) says, "Seek the Lord and his strength; seek his presence continually!" It's You, Lord Jesus, that I will look to when I need strength. When I need peace or joy, all these things can only be found in Your presence. Your Word in Proverbs 8:17 (ESV) says, "I love those who love me, and those who seek me diligently find me." Father, I confess my love for You today, and I hold on to this promise of Yours that if I seek You diligently, I will find You. I pray that my appetite for Godly things will grow day by day. Let me always be hungry for Your presence. Let me always be thirsty for fellowship with You, King Jesus. If I seek You first, I can find everything else that I want and need in You. In You, Lord, there is protection, because Your Word tells me that no weapon formed against me shall prosper. No weapon from the enemy will destroy me, for the God of the heavens is my deliverer.

Lord Jesus, You are ever faithful. You are my hiding place. Your Word says that Your plans for me are good, plans to give me a hope and a future. I will trust in You. When I have questions, You have the answers. I don't know what I will face in the future, but I will seek You, Lord. You are a God who holds the future, the present, and the past in His hands. Whatever is unknown to me in the future, I have confidence that it will work out for my good, because You are already there and You have already made a way. You are a God who will never leave me, or forsake me.

Your Word tells me that You are a stronghold in the day of trouble. You're my refuge and my strength. You're the Lion of the tribe of Judah. Father, I ask for divine protection. I ask for divine provision. Lord, I will seek You with all my heart, mind, and soul because l need your presence to be with me. May I see Your hand moving in my life despite present circumstances. Lord, You are my refuge and strength, an ever-present help in trouble. Be blessed and glorified.

In the name of Jesus Christ l pray

Amen.

DO NOT BE TROUBLED

We all face troubling circumstances every now and again. In this life there will be things, events, and words spoken to and against us that will either hurt us or leave us feeling discouraged. However, there is comfort in the Lord. There is hope and healing in Jesus Christ.

John 14:1 (AMP) states, "Do not let your heart be troubled (afraid, cowardly). Believe [confidently] in God and trust in Him, [have faith, hold on to it, rely on it, keep going and] believe also in Me."

In Jesus Christ, you should see yourself living free from depression, from guilt, from shame, and from condemnation! In Jesus, you should see yourself living free from anxiety and stress. Our Lord and Saviour Jesus Christ has said to us, "Do not let your heart be troubled..." How many of us obey this instruction? How many of us choose faith over fear? How many of us choose to trust in the Lord over focusing on our troubles? In Jesus Christ, you have peace, refuge and certain victory. So, if your heart is troubled today, take your burdens to the Redeemer. Take that which bothers you and lay it before the Lord. Take everything to Jesus; the pain from any stinging criticism, the pain from betrayal, or the pain of disappointments. Take it all to Jesus Christ.

Psalm 147:3 (ESV) says, "He heals the brokenhearted and binds up their wounds." There's no pit so deep that God can't lift you out of and dust you off. There is nothing so dark that God's light can't shine into! So do not let your heart be troubled. Invite the Lord into your circumstances.

PRAYER

My dear Father,

You are a holy God. Your love is unending and Your love is awesome. I pray that You will heal me, Lord. Mend my broken heart. Let me not be disheartened. Let me not be discouraged. Fill me with Your joy. Strengthen me with Your joy, Father, because Your Word says in Nehemiah 8:10 (NKJV), "...Do not sorrow, for the joy of the Lord is your strength." Be with me, Lord, and give me the strength to endure the trials I face King Jesus. John 14:1 (NIV) says, "Do not let your hearts be troubled. You believe in God; believe also in me." I receive Your words Lord. My heart is not troubled, because I belong to God Almighty. I pray that Your peace will rest upon my life. I pray for a peace that is beyond all understanding, a heavenly peace, to rest over me and cover my emotions, my soul, and for it to dwell in my spirit.

Your Word says that weeping endures for a night, but joy comes in the morning. My hope is within You, God, and I look to You as the anchor of my soul. Lord, flood every corner of my emotions. May the blood of Jesus remove every negative thought. You are the Good Shepherd. You are the healer of broken hearts. I call on Your great goodness and abundant grace. May it overflow in my life.

Your Word tells me to come to you when I am weary, and You will give me rest. Father, I hold on to Your Word and promises because You say that You honour Your Word to us even above Your name. Flood my heart and mind with Your love. Refresh my weary and burdened soul. Strengthen me in my weakness. Help me in my turmoil and heal my hurting heart, Lord Jesus. Your Word says that You heal the broken-hearted, and You are near to those who are downcast and depressed. I pray that when the storms of life are raging, Your presence will calm the rough waters, no matter the circumstance, no matter the situation. You are the rock of all ages, my strong tower and fortress. When I grow tired and weary, when I stumble and fall, I pray that Your strength will renew me. I pray that your presence would forever be with me and continuously surrounding me. You are a faithful God, and I thank You in advance for being my light in the darkest of hours.

In the mighty name of Jesus Christ I pray,

Amen.

SURRENDER TO GOD

Psalm 34:18 (AMP)
"The Lord is near to the heartbroken and
He saves those who are crushed in spirit
(contrite in heart, truly sorry for their sin)."

Brokenness is a necessary attribute for a believer. It must be found in our character as Christians. The Bible tells us that God is near to the broken-hearted. One may ask, what is it to be broken-hearted? Or, what is brokenness? Brokenness is not about having your heart crushed or suffering a mental breakdown. Rather, brokenness is being grieved by the awareness that our sin separates us from God. Its being crushed in spirit at the realization that Jesus Christ paid a heavy price for me to have eternal life, and the sin in my life is an act of disregard to the work of Christ.

Being broken, surrendered, and crushed in spirit is going before God with a repentant and sorrowful heart, because we know that the wages of sin is death, and that "death" is to be separated from God's presence for eternity. A person who is fully surrendered to God and broken seeks not only forgiveness but renewal, a new way of living that will please God, a new way of thinking that pleases God. This is a process that brings you to totally trust and submit to the Lord. It's only when we reach such a state that we'll find Him to be a God who will smooth "all uneven edges" and, like an expert Potter, He will begin to mould you into the man or woman you were called to be.

Hebrews 12:5 (NKJV) says, "And you have forgotten the exhortation which speaks to you as to sons: 'My son, do not despise the chastening of the Lord, nor be discouraged when you are rebuked by Him.'" The process of brokenness in our lives means that our personal pride must be removed. Our will has to go, and instead, our cry becomes, "Thy will be done, O Lord." Brokenness must never be avoided by us as believers. We instead need to embrace it, because it produces a Godly character and "good fruit" in our lives. It brings about growth and maturity. Genuine prayer only happens when it's coming from someone truly striving to live a clean life and has a broken heart over their sin. We should all have an attitude of self-denial that says, "Your will be done, O Lord, Your name be lifted high." It's from this stance that we should pray. A place where we realise that it is absolutely necessary for us to approach God with humility and brokenness of heart, because we deserve nothing. Yet if we repent, we can receive forgiveness and eternal life through Jesus Christ.

PRAYER

My Heavenly Father,

I come in the name of Jesus Christ, the name that was given power above every other name. I bow down to you King Jesus Christ of Nazareth. I submit completely to You, Lord. Thank You for Your love. Thank You for Your mercies, which are new every morning. Thank You for Your power that wakes me up every morning. Thank You for strengthening me throughout the day.

I commit and surrender myself totally and completely into Your hands, Lord. I pray that you would mould me, and make me the best that I can be for You. Fill me up to overflow according to Your will, O God. I want to be more like You, Father. Make me a true ambassador with a burden to represent You to the whole world by spreading the gospel of Jesus Christ. I pray, Father, for the boldness to preach Jesus to others. I pray that my thoughts, my words, and my intentions may be pure and pleasing to You. Fill me up with Your spirit and let my life be totally consumed by Your power.

Holy Spirit, I invite You to come into my heart. I pray that, just like Paul, I may be crucified with Christ and no longer live but have Christ live in me. I pray, Lord Jesus, that Your grace, favour, and love will be upon me each and every day. I pray, Father God, that I may be completely subdued and humbled before You, O Lord. May all my prayers, motives, deeds, and conduct be to Your glory. I pray that my thoughts, my words, and my intentions be pure and pleasing to You. I thank

You for Your Word which says that You do not delight in sacrifices or with burnt offerings, but You desire a broken spirit, a broken and a contrite heart. Father, may I always be broken before You. May I have a humble and willing spirit each time that I come before You.

I pray that through the brokenness of my heart, my life will be transformed for the good and benefit of the kingdom of God. Help me, Lord, to have the attitude of self-denial that says, "More of You and less of me." Let Your will be done in my life.

I pray, Father God, that my life may be fertile ground, ready to produce kingdom fruits, fruits of love, peace, long-suffering, and joy. I pray for a humble attitude. Your Word says that You are near to those who have a broken heart, may this become my lifestyle. Let it not be a one-off experience, but let brokenness be the condition of my heart.

Lord, Your word says in Hebrews 4:16 (NKJV), "Let us therefore come boldly to the throne of grace, that we may obtain mercy and find grace to help in time of need." Lord 1 am at Your mercy. I am asking that You would begin to work within me and turn my heart of stone into a heart that is sensitive and yielded to Your will. Give me a heart that is not self-serving but one that seeks to please you, day after day. Let there be no love for sin in my heart, King Jesus. Instead, stir up my spirit so that 1 will hunger and thirst for Your presence.

Father, cleanse me with the blood of Jesus Christ. Remove any pride from within me. Remove all selfishness. Help me to be someone who simply longs to serve you. I thank You, Lord, for Your faithfulness. I bless Your holy name. Thank You for hearing this prayer

In the name of Jesus Christ 1 pray,

Amen.

INVITE THE HOLY SPIRIT

The wonderful thing about the Holy Spirit is that He brings individuals to a place of complete and total trust in Jesus Christ. The Holy Spirit unites us with the Lord and provides us with access to so many wonderful benefits that come as a result of accepting Christ into our hearts.

Acts 2:38 (NKJV) reads, "Then Peter said to them, 'Repent, and let every one of you be baptized in the name of Jesus Christ for the remission of sins; and you shall receive the gift of the Holy Spirit.' " The Holy Spirit is referred to as a gift. He is a wonderful gift from God to us believers. He is a gift because you will not find a better helper on this earth than the Holy Ghost. He enables us to do the right thing. He convicts us to repent and turn away from sin. The Holy Spirit strengthens us in the Lord. He empowers us to pray and have faith. The Holy Spirit is a teacher, He reveals the Word of God to us and gives us understanding and insight.

Luke 12:12 (NKJV) declares, "For the Holy Spirit will teach you in that very hour what you ought to say." There are so many blessings that come with the Holy Spirit. When you are trapped by temptation, He will come to your rescue and empower you to overcome. If you feel empty, if you feel as though there is a void in your life, invite the Holy Spirit into your heart. In the lives of many believers, the lack of understanding about the Holy Spirit and his role in our lives is the missing link to an effective and fruitful walk with Christ.

John 16:13 (ESV) says, "When the Spirit of truth comes, he will guide you into all the truth, for he will not speak on his own authority, but whatever he hears he will speak, and he will declare to you the things that are to come." We need the Holy Spirit because He guides us into all truth. The Bible teaches us that Jesus is the truth, for Jesus says, "I am the way, the truth, and the life." The Holy Spirit will guide you to Jesus Christ. The Holy Spirit will reveal Jesus Christ to you. The Holy Spirit will enable you to seek the Lord wholeheartedly. This is why we absolutely need the Holy Spirit in our lives.

PRAYER

Heavenly Father,

You are the One who sustains me. You are my provider. I humbly enter Your presence seeking Your forgiveness, seeking for You to cleanse me, for I am a sinner. I repent and I ask for the blood of Jesus Christ to wash me clean so that the Holy Spirit can dwell within me. I recognize that I need the gift of the Holy Spirit. Fill me with Your Holy Spirit so that I can have a closer walk with You. I desire to know Your will and to be filled with Godly desires in my life. Your Word says that no one knows the thoughts of God except through the Spirit of God. Reveal to me Your will for my life through the Holy Spirit. I pray that the Holy Spirit would reveal You more to me each and every day. May the Holy Spirit show me Your way. May He guide me into all truth, even in times of doubts and confusion.

I pray that Your Spirit of Truth will rule over my life. I pray for the spirit of discernment so that I may not believe the lies of the devil. Help me to identify deception and to only be sensitive to the things of God.

When the devil wants me to believe that I will never overcome the challenge before me, may the Spirit of God remind me that Romans 8:37-39 (NIV) says, "37 No, in all these things we are more than conquerors through him who loved us. 38 For I am convinced that neither death nor life, neither angels nor demons, neither the present nor the future, nor any powers, 39 neither height nor depth, nor anything else in all creation, will be able to separate us from the love of God that is in Christ Jesus our Lord." Set me free, O God, from the lies and misconceptions of this world. I pray that I may always be inspired and led by Your Spirit of Truth. Holy Spirit, I desire to live a life that is pure and holy in the sight of God. I cannot do it alone. Light a fire in my soul for Jesus Christ. Holy Spirit, stir up my spirit so that I can chase the Lord with desperation.

Empower me, Lord Jesus, so that I may be able to rise above this life of sin. Renew me, sanctify me, and make me clean so that I can live a life that is pleasing to you. Remove impure desires. Turn my heart away from the lust of the flesh. Turn my heart away from the lust of the eyes and the pride of life.

The Bible says in Romans 8:26 (NKJV), "Likewise the Spirit also helps in our weaknesses. For we know not what we should pray for as we ought, but the Spirit Himself makes intercession for us with groanings which cannot be uttered." If I am too weak to pray, intercede on my behalf Holy Spirit, step in and be My Helper.

Lord, I want to bear good fruit in my life. I want to have a character that is loving, humble, and peaceful. I invite you to be with me always Holy Spirit.

I thank you for hearing my prayer.

In the mighty name of Jesus Christ I pray,

Amen.

RAISING YOUR HANDS IN BATTLE

What do you do when you get into a fight? Not a physical fight, but the kind of fight that Daniel got into when he prayed for 21 days. It's the kind of fight that Jesus found himself in when He was fasting for 40 days and 40 nights. Those are real fights.

In Exodus 17, Moses and Joshua found themselves in a fight against Amalek. However, this fight, although physical, was to be won or lost through prayer. The outcome of this fight was to be determined by prayer. Exodus 17:11-13 (AMP) says, "11 Now when Moses held up his hand, Israel prevailed, and when he lowered his hand [due to fatigue], Amalek prevailed. 12 But Moses' hands were heavy and he grew tired. So they took a stone and put it under him, and he sat on it. Then Aaron and Hur held up his hands, one on one side and one on the other side; so it was that his hands were steady until the sun set. 13 So Joshua overwhelmed and defeated Amalek and his people with the edge of the sword."

During the last fight you were in, did you consider raising up your hands? During the fight you are currently in, have you considered raising up your hands? When it comes to any fight that you will face in the future, will you consider raising up your hands and acknowledging God in the midst of a difficult situation? When a man or woman of God raises up their hands in a battle, in a spiritual battle, they are surrendering the fight to the Lord.

Exodus 14:14 (NKJV) says, "The Lord will fight for you, and you shall hold your peace." What does that tell you? It tells you that the battle is not yours! This battle you face should be fought with hands raised in prayer, because it's a battle that you are surrendering to a higher authority! Raising your hands in thanksgiving and praise is another key to victory in a battle. Ask Paul and Silas. They'll tell you all about how raised hands in worship and praise can invoke the mighty power of God!

Psalm 150:6 (NIV) commands, "Let everything that has breath praise the Lord. Praise the Lord." Worship the Lord today. Give Him your praise and your adoration. Give thanks for all that He has done, for all that He is doing, and in faith, for all that He will do.

PRAYER

Heavenly Father,

I thank You for Your protection. I praise You for Your goodness. I pray that Your presence will always surround me. May Your divine peace always be found in my mind and in my heart. I lay my burdens at Your feet Lord Jesus. I pray that the Holy Spirit would help me not to let the worries and cares of this world to pull me down. Help me not to hold on to anything painful from the past. I pray that you would give me peace and take away every unsettling thing. Give me joy and remove everything that troubles my heart.

In those moments when I feel low, or even if I am disappointed, may You lift my burdens and give me strength. I worship You, King Jesus, because when I'm in need, You are my provider. You're the rock of all ages, my stronghold, and my fortress. You are my source of joy and strength when I am discouraged, tired, and weary. I know I can always find comfort in You. Renew my strength, as I look to You, Lord Jesus. I invite Your presence because only in You can I find a deep sense of peace.

I look to You Lord. I look to You for guidance, for direction and instruction. I will not lean on my own understanding, because I am limited. Instead, I will lean on Your Word and trust that it will be a lamp to my feet.

Your Word in Isaiah 43:2 (NIV) says, "When you pass through the waters, I will be with you; and when you pass through the rivers, they will not sweep over you. When you walk through the fire, you will not be burned; the flames will not set you ablaze."

In Your Word, I place my confidence, Lord. In Your Word, I place my hope and faith for tomorrow. I'm grateful for Your protection, for Your provision in my life, Lord Jesus. Thank You for the amazing grace that is over me and my family. You are a God who has been faithful throughout the ages and I praise You.

Lord Jesus, I thank You for Your faithfulness. Thank You for being my light, even in the darkest of times. I thank You for being the solid rock that I can stand on whenever I feel as though I am sinking in this world. I praise You for being the Good Shepherd that guides me daily.

Lord Jesus, at this time, I ask for joy. I pray for supernatural joy that comes only from You, Lord, so that I may not be disheartened when things don't go my way. Help me not to be discouraged by the disappointments of life, but rather, let the joy of the Lord be my strength. I pray that the Holy Spirit would help me to focus on You, Lord Jesus, and not my problems. Holy Spirit, help me to worship instead of worry, to rejoice rather than to fall into despair.

I praise You, Lord Jesus, for Your love is unending. My faith is assured because of You. My faith is anchored in You, for You have control over all things. Thank You for being a refuge and strong tower, a very present help in times of trouble. Be glorified, Lord.

In Jesus' name I pray,

Amen.

HOPE AND STRENGTH

There are situations in life that will break you if you do not hold on to the word of God. The problems of life can be overwhelming when you try and tackle them with your own strength and resources. As believers, the trials and challenges we face in life can really only be won when we have accepted that in our weakness, God's strength is magnified. However, you may be asking the question, "How do I gain hope and strength in God when the trouble before me is so real, when it's so painful? How do I continue to truly hope in the Lord and be strengthened by the Lord, when my burdens are so heavy and when they are so many?"

Well, the Bible is filled with promises that serve to inspire, strengthen, and give us hope. In God's word, we can find promises that will shine a light into what is seemingly a dark situation. Some of the key scriptures to remember, meditate, and dwell on when things are difficult are:

Deuteronomy 31:6 (NKJV) "Be strong and of good courage, do not fear nor be afraid of them; for the Lord your God, He is the One who goes with you. He will not leave you nor forsake you."

Philippians 4:7 (NIV) "And the peace of God, which transcends all understanding, will guard your hearts and your minds in Christ Jesus."

2 Corinthians 5:7 (ESV) "for we walk by faith, not by sight."

Psalm 23:5-6 (NKJV) "You prepare a table before me in the presence of my enemies; you anoint my head with oil; my cup runs over. Surely goodness and mercy shall follow me all the days of my life; and I will dwell in the house of the Lord forever."

Mark 11:22-24 (NKJV) "So Jesus answered and said to them, 'Have faith in God. For assuredly, I say to you, whoever says to this mountain, "Be removed and be cast into the sea," and does not doubt in his heart, but believes that those things he says will be done, he will have whatever he says. Therefore I say to you, whatever things you ask when you pray, believe that you receive them, and you will have them."

Proverbs 3:5-6 (NKJV) "Trust in the Lord with all your heart, and lean not on your own understanding; in all your ways acknowledge Him, and He shall direct your paths."

Psalm 28:7 (NIV) "The Lord is my strength and my shield; my heart trusts in him, and he helps me. My heart leaps for joy, and with my song I praise him."

PRAYER

Dear Lord,

I pray that You will give me the grace to rise up each day and live a life that is pleasing to You. Give me the strength, Father God, to fight against the temptations and forces of this world.

Holy Spirit, You are welcome. I invite You into my heart. I invite You into my day. May You strengthen my faith. When the tests and trials of this life begin to feel overwhelming, remind me that I have a friend "who sticks closer than a brother," according to Proverbs 18:24 (NKJV).

In You, King Jesus, I have safe refuge. I am kept, sustained and led by You, Lord. You are my rescue in my hour of need, and I am grateful because Your love is stronger and purer than anything on this earth.

Father, when my problems are many and they seek to overwhelm me, I pray that the Holy Spirit will remind me that I serve a living God who is more than able to carry my burdens. I know that You are an all-powerful God. There is nothing that is too difficult for You. Lord, I praise You for Your consistency. You are the same yesterday, today, and forevermore. You still move mountains, and You still cause walls to fall. There is nothing too big for You, and I rejoice because of your might and power.

I pray that other people will look at my life and see Your goodness. May they see Your mercy and Your power. May unbelievers in this world see Your miraculous hand when they see me, Father. May they see Your love for someone who was lost but is now found. May they see Your forgiveness for a sinner such as me. May they see Your divine strength in my weakness. I pray that every lost soul I encounter sees evidence of a merciful God, a God who has amazing grace that saved a wretch like me.

Psalm 32:7 (ESV) says, "You are a hiding place for me; you preserve me from trouble; you surround me with shouts of deliverance." I praise You for such a promise. A promise that gives me hope and strength despite the battles l face. Your Word says in Luke 10:19 (NKJV), "Behold, I give you the authority to trample on serpents and scorpions, and over all the power of the enemy, and nothing shall by any means hurt you." I thank You, King Jesus, for this authority that You have given me to overcome all the power of the enemy. I stand and declare that nothing will harm me. Nothing will harm my loved ones and my family, in Jesus' name. The devil has no authority over my home. He has no say over my future or my family. He has no power over my health in Jesus' name.

I trust in You, Jehovah. I say that You are my refuge. You are the chief cornerstone. I choose to trust in the true and living God.

Help me not to fear but to trust You. Help me not to be discouraged but to have joy in You. Help me not to take Your goodness and kindness for granted. I declare my faith in Your ability to fulfil Your promises to me. You will fight for me and win the battles in my life. You are mighty, powerful, righteous, and true.

Father, the Bible tells me that my words are powerful and that the tongue can speak life or death. Lord, I declare that I am strong and courageous in the Lord. I pray and declare that I am protected by the blood of King Jesus Christ. I have nothing to fear because the Lord is by my side. I have nothing to fear because God has not given me a spirit of fear but of power, and of love, and of a sound mind. I declare that nothing will destroy me. I will not be crushed by any challenge I face. I will not be destroyed by any situation or burden. I stand in faith, as I look to King Jesus Christ, my Saviour, my help, a stronghold in the day of trouble.

I bless and honour Your Holy name Lord Jesus,

Amen.

TOMORROW IS NOT PROMISED

James 4:14 (NKJV)
"whereas you do not know what will happen tomorrow.
For what is your life? It is even a vapour that appears
for a little time and then vanishes away."

Think about that. For you are a vapour, the Bible says. In the grand scheme of eternity, you appear for a little time and then you vanish. Tomorrow is not promised. Tomorrow is not in our hands. At any given moment, the Lord could call us home.

Are you living your life with an urgency for the things of Christ? Because if you truly believe that tomorrow is not promised, then you will live with a purpose. Everything you do should be done with a view of eternity. Everything you work towards should be done with a view of eternity. With each passing second, each minute, and every hour, we are edging closer to an appointed time when we will stand before God and give an account for what we've done with our lives.

So now is the time to get right and build a close relationship with Jesus Christ. Now is the time to work and to serve the kingdom of God. Now is the time to fully surrender to Jesus Christ.

Don't put it off a second longer. There's no reason to wait. There is joy in Him. There is eternal life in Him.

When you stop wrestling with God and let Him transform your life, you will experience a freedom like you've never felt before. Jesus satisfies every hunger. He quenches every thirst. He fills the deepest longings of your soul. So come to Him today.

The Lord is patient and willing to forgive those who come to him with a broken and contrite heart. Hebrews 9:27 (NKJV) says, "And as it is appointed for men to die once, but after this the judgment." With this in mind, I encourage you to live with an urgency. Time is ticking. Sooner or later, either you will stand before the Lord in an instant, or He will return to take his church away. Either way, time is ticking.

You and I need to live a life that is mindful of the fact that we will all be accountable for what we did for Jesus and what we didn't do. Will you be able to say that your life produced good fruit for the Kingdom of God? Will you be able to say that during your days here on earth, you had eternity on your mind?

Far too many people waste their lives on things that won't last: money, power, relationships. But God is not concerned with those things. He is concerned with the state of your heart. What matters is how you live your life in accordance to God's Word. What matters is did you put Jesus Christ first? What matters is who lives on the throne of your heart.

At the end of your life, the Lord will not ask how much money you made, He won't ask you how many friends you made, or even how many good works you did. He will simply want to know who you trusted for your eternal salvation. Who did you serve? Who did you love with all your heart, with all your mind and soul?

The only correct answer, in fact the only answer is Jesus Christ, the Son of God.

PRAYER

Lord Jesus,

I thank You for Your love. I thank You for Your saving grace.

Your love, Lord Jesus Christ, is all encompassing. It's a love that has accepted me in my sinful state and called me to repentance. Thank You for Your mercy. Your mercy has afforded me the opportunity to enter eternal life. Your mercy has saved me from eternal damnation. Because of Your mercy, Lord, I can look forward to everlasting joy in Your presence.

Titus 2:11-14 (ESV) reads:

> [11] *For the grace of God has appeared, bringing salvation for all people,* [12] *training us to renounce ungodliness and worldly passions, and to live self-controlled, upright, and godly lives in the present age,* [13] *waiting for our blessed hope, the appearing of the glory of our great God and*

Savior Jesus Christ, [14] who gave himself for us to redeem us from all lawlessness and to purify for himself a people for his own possession who are zealous for good works.

King Jesus, You are my blessed hope.

Lord, help me to live a Godly life in this present evil age. In this age, where sin is rampant, where the love of many has grown cold, I pray that the Holy Spirit will keep the fire of Christ burning brightly in my heart. Help me, Holy Spirit, not to grow cold or lukewarm when it comes to all things concerning Jesus Christ. Help me not to be tempted or lured into the ways of this world. Give me the grace and strength I need to live a life that is upright and pure. Help me to live a life that demonstrates the love of Jesus Christ to all people, saved or unsaved. Let my life be a living example, a living testimony, of God's amazing grace and eternal mercies.

Father, in and among all of the distractions in this world, I pray that my focus will only be on You. Let my heart always be filled with the hopeful expectation of Your return, Lord Jesus.

Your Word says in Mark 13:32-33 (NIV) "But about that day or hour no one knows, not even the angels in heaven, nor the Son, but only the Father. Be on guard! Be alert! You do not know when that time will come."

Father, I pray that I will always be on guard against the deceptions and distractions of this world. Help me to always be alert that You could return at any time, Lord.

Or You could call me home at any time. Either way, Father, as Your Word says in Philippians 1:21 (NKJV), "For to me, to live is Christ, and to die is gain."

King Jesus, it is my heart's desire to spend eternity with You. It is my heart's desire to live this life for Your glory. Holy Spirit, will you continually help me to walk on the narrow path and carry my cross so that one day I can be in my Saviour's presence forever and ever.

I praise your name, King Jesus, and I thank you for listening to my prayer.

Be glorified.

In Jesus' name I pray,

Amen.

NO LONGER BOUND

If you feel as though you are bound or restricted in any area of your life, I want you to know that Jesus Christ can set you free. Jesus Christ can break every chain in your life.

The enemy has a strategy in place against us as the children of God. The devil seeks to oppress, to bind, to limit and to restrict. However, when God gets involved, He brings freedom, He brings liberty, He restores and makes you whole again. When God gets involved in your affairs and in your situation, He releases you from all limitations and restrictions.

Luke 13:10-13 (ESV) says:

> *10 Now he was teaching in one of the synagogues on the Sabbath. 11 And behold, there was a woman who had had a disabling spirit for eighteen years. She was bent over and could not fully straighten herself. 12 When Jesus saw her, he called her over and said to her, "Woman, you are freed from your disability." 13 And he laid his hands on her, and immediately she was made straight, and she glorified God.*

Let's focus on verse 12. "When Jesus saw her, he called her over and said to her, 'Woman, you are freed from your disability.' "

Now this woman was freed from her disability. What's interesting here is that the Bible says she was freed from her disability and not healed. It's as if Jesus was saying to her "you are no longer confined or imprisoned by your disability." This is what Jesus Christ offers us... freedom. Freedom from oppression, freedom from sin and death.

I encourage you to believe that Jesus Christ can set you free. He can set you free from depression and anxiety. He can set you free from that secret addiction. He can set you free from the anger and resentment hidden in your heart. Jesus Christ can set you free from everything that limits and restricts you.

You are not bound to that situation, because God can turn any situation around. You are not enslaved by the forces of evil, because Jesus Christ has defeated the devil, He has defeated hell and all of its forces.

I love what the Bible says in Luke 4:17-19 (NKJV):

> *17 And He was handed the book of the prophet Isaiah. And when He had opened the book, He found the place where it was written: 18 "The Spirit of the Lord is upon Me, Because He has anointed Me to preach the gospel to the poor; He has sent Me to heal the brokenhearted, to proclaim liberty to the captives and recovery of sight to*

the blind, to set at liberty those who are oppressed; [19] to proclaim the acceptable year of the Lord."

In Jesus there is healing for the broken-hearted so that they are no longer held hostage by the pain of yesterday. In Jesus there is liberty for the captives so that they are no longer condemned by their sins but they are forgiven because of the wonderful work of Jesus Christ on the cross.

Be encouraged, if you are seeking freedom, seek Jesus.

PRAYER

My heavenly Father, my Lord and Saviour, Jesus Christ,

I come to You today with a humble spirit. I come to You with a heart filled with faith and expectation. You are a God who can bind up all of my wounds. Because of You, Lord, I am no longer a slave to sin. Because of You, I am no longer captive to the forces of evil.

I declare Your Word which tells me that greater is He who is in me than he who is in the world! Meaning that You, King Jesus, have placed within me, the strength to overcome adversity, the strength to overcome the devil and for that I rejoice and I thank You, Lord!

I thank You, because in You I can walk in victory and I have the power to defeat sin. This is all because of You, and I am grateful. Because of who You are, Lord, I bow down and glorify You, I humble myself and surrender all that I am to You. I trust and believe that You will liberate me, You will redeem me, and You will make me whole again.

I pray for freedom in all areas of my life. Freedom from any strongholds, any chains that seek to hold me back or hold me down. Give me freedom in my mind, Lord, freedom from the guilt of past sins and past mistakes.

Your Word in Isaiah 43:18 (NKJV) says, "Do not remember the former things, nor consider the things of old."

Help me to let go and forget the former things. King Jesus give me the grace not to dwell on the past. Help me to look forward, to look forward to You doing a new thing in my life. Help me to look forward to a life of freedom in Jesus Christ.

Father, I need You to set me free from everything that seeks to bind me or my family. I need divine intervention. Help me to let go of everything that weighs me down or tries to limit my belief. Lord, help me to let go of the past and let go of any pain, anger, and shame from the past. Help me to forgive anyone who has disappointed or betrayed me.

Holy Spirit, I pray that You will soften my heart so that I will never be hardened with resentment, bitterness or unforgiveness. God, I come to You seeking healing in Your arms. Make me whole again. Give me the strength to let go and move on from the past.

Lord God, I look forward to a future with You. I embrace a future that is in Your hands, one that is filled with love, mercy, and goodness.

As I reach out in prayer, I put my hopes and dreams, my plans and relationships in Your hands. With You by my side, there is nothing that can hold me back.

I thank You for freedom, Master.

In the mighty name of Jesus Christ I pray,

Amen.

YOU ARE STRONG EVEN WHEN YOU ARE WEAK

We all have different stories to tell when it comes to some of the events that have transpired in our lives. Some of us have really experienced dark moments. We've lived through days where it felt as though the weight of the entire world was on our shoulders. For others, we've felt as though we've hit rock bottom, and we were isolated and forgotten even.

However, when life brings you to your knees that's when you are at your strongest, and you're at your strongest because you have done all you can. You've exhausted your own resources, and you're now at a place where you have nothing else to give.

When you reach this point, when life has brought you to your knees, this is when you must come to the same realization that Paul came to in 2 Corinthians 12:9-10 (ESV). The Bible reads, "But he said to me, 'My grace is sufficient for you, for my power is made perfect in weakness.' Therefore I will boast all the more gladly of my weaknesses, so that the power of Christ may rest upon me. For the sake of Christ, then, I am content with weaknesses, insults, hardships, persecutions, and calamities. For when I am weak, then I am strong."

It's in your weakest moment that God's strength is magnified! It's in your darkest moment that the light of Jesus Christ shines the brightest. It's only when you've reached your limit that you can truly understand how limitless our God is.

Whatever you're facing, God's grace is sufficient for you. Whatever challenge you're facing, God's power is made perfect in your weakness. If you feel as though you have hit rock bottom, God's loving-kindness and His mercy are more than enough to see you through. So, child of God, don't give up. Whatever hardship you face, don't give up. Should you feel outnumbered and overwhelmed, don't give up because when you are weak that's when God's strength is best demonstrated.

Now, when you look through the Bible, you will find stories of people who, in their weakness, demonstrated incredible, supernatural strength because, at the end of their limitations, God took over.

David couldn't defeat Goliath on his own, God took over. The three Hebrew boys, Shadrach, Meshach, and Abednego, couldn't withstand a fiery furnace. God took over. The walls of Jericho came down because God took over. Moses and the children of Israel couldn't cross the Red Sea until God took over. The woman with the issue of blood couldn't be healed until God took over.

All of these people faced different situations and they were all limited in some way. They all had their weaknesses, but it was at their weakest moments that God's strength was magnified.

And so here's what I would like to tell you. Let God take over your situation. In your weakness, let God's strength be magnified. Remember that in His Word, God has said, "My grace is sufficient for you…" and "…my power is made perfect in weakness." Believe!

PRAYER

Lord Jesus,

Be glorified. Be praised.

Father, with You on my side, I will all the more gladly boast in my weaknesses. Lord, when I feel overwhelmed, when I feel powerless, Your Word in Philippians 4:13 (ESV) says, "I can do all things through him who strengthens me."

You are my source of strength. You are my source of power, Father, and I look to You for divine intervention when I am faced with difficulties. There is nothing impossible with You, Lord Jesus.

When I am limited, Your Word in Philippians 4:19 (ESV) says, "And my God will supply every need of yours according to his riches in glory in Christ Jesus."

You, Lord, are rich in power. You are rich in wisdom, and there is nothing too difficult for You. Father, You have solutions for anything and everything I could face in this world. You have answers far beyond the resources of any expert, or any doctor, in this world.

Your ways, God, are far above and far higher than ours.

Psalm 40:1-2 (NKJV) says: " ¹ I waited patiently for the Lord; And He inclined to me, and heard my cry. ² He also brought me up out of a horrible pit, out of the miry clay, and set my feet upon a rock, and established my steps."

I pray that You will hear my cry, Lord Jesus. When my heart is troubled, when I am weak, when I feel threatened by the enemy, hear my cry Lord. Set my feet on higher ground and establish my steps. Whatever challenges may come my way, let me not be daunted and apprehensive. Give me a spirit of boldness. Help me to realize that when I have reached my breaking point, You are the one who not only holds me together but You give me the strength to overcome.

I invite You into my life, Lord. I invite You into my situation. Deliver me from my troubles. Fight on my behalf, Lord. Make a way for me where there seems to be no way. Give me the faith to withstand every fiery trial I face. Give me the grace to overcome any persecution I may face.

Lord, in all that I do, as I strive to be more and more like You each day, give me the strength to fight and persevere. Give me the strength to resist the devil, the strength to fight this flesh and my carnal, sinful nature. Give me the strength, Lord, to stand and remain anchored in Your Word even when this world offers me many temptations.

Your Word in Romans 8:26 (ESV) says, "Likewise the Spirit helps us in our weakness. For we do not know what to pray for as we ought, but the Spirit himself intercedes for us with groanings too deep for words."

Help me in my weakness, Holy Spirit. When I am unable to pray, when I am struggling with all that has come against me, Holy Spirit, may You intercede on my behalf.

Lord Jesus, I bless Your precious name. Thank You for hearing my prayer.

In Jesus' name I pray,

Amen.

MY GREAT DEFENDER

2 Thessalonians 3:3 (NIV)
"But the Lord is faithful, and he will strengthen you
and protect you from the evil one."

God, in His faithfulness, has promised to protect us from the evil one. On this topic of God's protection, I believe that, because God works in ways that we may not understand, His protection will not always be obvious to the naked eye. Of course, God protects us in the physical as well as the spiritual. However, I also believe that sometimes God's protection comes in the form of peace and strength in the middle of despair and chaos. Other times, God's protection can even come in the form of one door closing in our lives because He sees something beyond the horizon that we cannot see. At times, God protects us by not giving us what we want because the very thing that we desire, could prove to be a stumbling block when it comes to our faith and growth as a believer, in the long run.

Overall, we need to remember what 2 Thessalonians 3:3 (NIV) says, "But the Lord is faithful, and he will strengthen you and protect you from the evil one."

The bottom line is that the Lord is faithful. He is so faithful that He neither sleeps nor slumbers, because He is watching over us. God is so faithful that even the very hairs on your head are all numbered. He is so faithful that before you were formed in your mother's womb... He knew you.

One passage of scripture that I would like to highlight is Revelation 5:5 (NIV), which reads: Then one of the elders said to me, "Do not weep! See, the Lion of the tribe of Judah, the Root of David, has triumphed. He is able to open the scroll and its seven seals."

I believe that this verse in Revelation is an important one to remember in our hearts.

When the bible says "Do not weep..." we're being told to stop worrying. Do not be discouraged because Jesus Christ has come out on top! The Lion of the tribe of Judah has prevailed.

Jesus Christ, the Lion of the tribe of Judah, the Root of David, has prevailed, He has mastered all things, He has won all battles, He is in command and He is victorious, and He will reign forever and ever.

When we think of protection, we ought to know who protects us. We ought to be aware of the might and power that the Lord has.

It's in Jesus Christ that we have our protection.

PRAYER

Lord Jesus,

I thank You for Your faithfulness. I thank You for Your divine protection. You are the God who defends me. You are the God who fights for me. You are the God who goes before me and surrounds me.

Your Word, in Psalm 125: 1-2 (ESV) says, "[1] Those who trust in the LORD are like Mount Zion, which cannot be moved, but abides forever. [2] As the mountains surround Jerusalem, so the LORD surrounds his people, from this time forth and forevermore."

I look to You, Father, because You are my defence. I pray that You will protect me in every storm and, if it is Your will, that I should endure any storm, then I pray that You would give me the grace and strength necessary to overcome.

Lord, I pray and I ask that You will protect me from the enemy so that he may never steal my joy or strength. Protect me, Father, and help me to guard my thoughts so that they may never be out of control and sinful. Let Your peace rule in my heart, and may Your angels encamp around me and around my home.

My God Jehovah, if You are my refuge, if You are my fortress, if You are for me, then who can be against me? All that I can ever need and desire can surely be found in You; a God who has proved himself throughout the ages to be neither weak nor mortal.

You are the Almighty one, and I can safely place my life in Your hands because I know that, in You, I will not be disappointed.

I praise You Lord, because no one can challenge You. You are without equal. You are unrivalled and unmatched.

I declare and decree Deuteronomy 28:6 over my life and say that, I will be blessed in my coming in and blessed in my going out, because you watch over me.

I declare Psalm 91:10 over my life and my family, and I say that no harm will overtake me, no disaster will come near my tent. No evil shall befall me, nor shall any plague come near my dwelling, in the name of Jesus Christ I pray.

I stand today in faith, covered by the power that's in the blood of Jesus Christ. I stand today concealed and wrapped by the blood of Jesus Christ which is miraculous and able to defeat all evil. I stand shielded and protected by the Holy Ghost.

You, Lord Jesus, are the Lion of the tribe of Judah, and I pray that You will defeat every demon from hell that is sent by the enemy to try and attack me. I pray that You will destroy every generational curse and every negative word spoken against me, in the mighty name of Jesus.

I pray that Your presence will always surround me, Lord.

Thank You for all of the goodness that You offer. I will continually place my trust in You.

Help me not to lean on my own understanding, because You are an all-knowing God, so my trust is in You.

I bless Your name, Lord Jesus. Thank You for Your wonderful love. I thank You for Your kindness, and I thank You for Your protection.

In the mighty and precious name of Jesus Christ,

Amen.

FREEDOM IN JESUS

The concept of freedom is mentioned several times in the Bible.

John 8:36 (ESV) "So if the Son sets you free, you will be free indeed."

Galatians 5:13 (ESV) "For you were called to freedom, brothers. Only do not use your freedom as an opportunity for the flesh, but through love serve one another."

Romans 6:18 (NLT) "Now you are free from your slavery to sin, and you have become slaves to righteous living."

Behind closed doors, most of us need to be set free from something. The pain of the past can become fertile ground that produces anger. Unforgiveness, which is secretly locked up in the heart, can hold you hostage and keep you from truly experiencing liberty and fulfilment in the Lord. Ungodly addictions can form strongholds of bondage. However, true and lasting freedom comes only from Jesus Christ. Should you make the decision today to surrender to the Son of God, should you choose to yield and welcome the

Holy Spirit, you will find that, in Jesus Christ, there is indeed freedom from bitterness and from any kind of addiction you may face. There is freedom from the guilt of previous sins if you truly repent. There is freedom from life's disappointments and rejections.

Psalm 118:5 (ESV) "Out of my distress I called on the Lord; the Lord answered me and set me free."

In your distress, you too can call on Jesus Christ, and He will set you free. He will break the chains in your life. He will unshackle you, leaving behind no trace of you ever having been a prisoner of the past or of sin. In the Lord, there is true, total, and complete freedom.

PRAYER

Dear Father,

My Lord and Saviour, Jesus Christ, I ask for freedom that comes only from You. I pray that You will set me free from the memory and guilt of the past. Release me from the bondage of past sins and even past mistakes. I ask that You set me free, Lord Jesus, because Your Word says in John 8:36 (NIV), "So if the Son sets you free, you will be free indeed."

Your Word in Isaiah 43:18 (ESV) says, "Remember not the former things, nor consider the things of old." Help me, Lord. Give me the grace not to dwell on the past. Help me to look forward, to look forward to You creating a new thing in my life. Free me from any scars, feelings of resentment, or bitterness from the past. I need divine intervention to help me let go of old habits, old patterns, and old disappointments. Help me to release the past and let go of pain and anger. Help me to forgive anyone who has ever hurt me, disappointed me, or betrayed me. Holy Spirit, help me to forgive and not to condemn. Father, help me to let go of traumatic experiences and help me to heal and move on. Give me freedom.

God, set me free from the pain and the memory of being mistreated. Set me free from being weighed down by heartbreak and loss. May Your love and compassion overwhelm me. May I find healing in Your arms. May I find wholeness in Your presence. And Lord, above all, may I find the strength to let go and move on from the past and enjoy true and lasting freedom in You. Your Word says in 2 Corinthians 3:17 (NIV), "Now the Lord is the Spirit, and where the Spirit of the Lord is, there is freedom." I invite You into my life, Lord. Only You can fully repair my heart, my mind, and my soul. Only You can give me closure where I need closure. Fill the voids that unsettle my heart, Lord Jesus.

Father, I look forward to a future with You. I embrace a future that is in Your hands, one that is filled with love, mercy, and goodness. As I reach out in prayer, I put my hopes and dreams, my plans and relationships in Your hands. With You by my side, the past will not hold me down, in Jesus' name. Sin will not hold me back, in Jesus' name. I declare that I have freedom in You, King Jesus, and the devil has no hold, no chain, or stronghold over me from today forward. I confess my sins, and I thank You for Your gracious mercy.

I pray that You will heal me, Lord. I ask that You release me from all feelings of condemnation and shame. Remove all feelings of guilt and destroy all bitterness. It's through Your redemptive blood that I can experience true and lasting freedom in my heart. I thank You for hearing my prayer, Lord.

In the mighty name of Jesus,

Amen.

STRONG FAITH

The Word of God teaches us that faith is absolutely necessary for a believer in Christ. It's through faith that we come to accept Jesus Christ as Our Lord and Saviour. It is also through faith that we live our lives with joy and gladness, knowing that there is eternity to be spent with the Father above.

The following passages of scripture underline just how much of a requirement faith is for the believer. It is the core of our Christian living.

Hebrews 11:6 (AMP), "But without faith it is impossible to [walk with God and] please Him, for whoever comes [near] to God must [necessarily] believe that God exists and that He rewards those who [earnestly and diligently] seek Him."

Matthew 21:22 (ESV), "And whatever you ask in prayer, you will receive, if you have faith."

Ephesians 2:8 (ESV), "For by grace you have been saved through faith. And this is not your own doing; it is the gift of God."

Hebrews 11:1 (ESV) reads, "Now faith is the assurance of things hoped for, the conviction of things not seen." The NKJV translation says, "Now faith is the substance of things hoped for, the evidence of things not seen."

Pay close attention to how the Bible describes faith:

1. Faith is assurance. It's a guarantee and a declaration of confidence in God's power and ability.

2. Faith is substance. It's real and tangible.

3. Faith is conviction. It's a firmly held belief, persuasion, or position in God. There is no doubt.

4. Faith is evidence. Faith is the proof, the indication, and the display of total trust in the Lord.

In a court of law, there will always be an argument put forward by each party. Both the prosecutor and defendant will have to provide evidence in order to persuade the court to find the case in their favour. It's the evidence that persuades the judge and the jury to come to a decision. So, if the Bible says that faith is the evidence of things not seen, that means that faith is us presenting our belief as evidence to God. So, when you say, "Lord, I trust in You to be my provider." How strong is your evidence? How strong is the belief you are presenting? When you say, "God, I trust You to be my healer." How robust is the case you're putting forward? Is it backed by layers and layers of faith? Is it backed by you waiting patiently for God to intervene, without murmuring or complaining? Is it backed by evidence such as you still having joy and praise in your heart, even though you are waiting for God to meet your need?

Faith is something that we should live with and exercise every single day. Faith should be the core principle that we stand on. We must walk by faith. Faith in God's Word, faith in who God is, and faith in His promises.

PRAYER

Heavenly Father,

I give You glory, and I give You praise. I pray that You will strengthen my faith, Lord. Increase and bolster my faith, King Jesus. Help me to trust like Job, so that if I were to lose everything, if my career was taken away from me, if my house and car were taken from me, I pray that I would still have unshakeable faith in you. I pray that I will always be able to declare the words in Job 13:15 (NKJV) and say, "Though He slay me, yet will I trust Him...."

God, I pray that I will have strong faith to be able to trust You regardless of my circumstances. Give me strong faith, so that when You speak to me and call me to do Your work, or when the time comes for me to step into my calling, I will not doubt or hesitate. Give me the faith to step out and walk on water. Father

I pray for bold faith that really understands that all things are possible with God. Give me faith to truly believe that You are the God of "I Am" and that You will make a way when there seems to be no way.

Lord, I pray for a heart of worship like David. I too want to chase after Your heart. I too want to worship You in spirit and in truth. Dear God, give me the boldness of the three Hebrew boys, the boldness to remove every idol in my life, the boldness to refuse to bow down to anything that tries to take Your place in my life.

Lord, I want to be obedient like Noah, so that when the naysayers come, when discouragers come my way, I may have the strength, belief, and conviction to obey You.

James 1:5 (NIV) says, "If any of you lacks wisdom, you should ask God, who gives generously to all without finding fault, and it will be given to you." Lord I pray that you will give me wisdom. Give me the wisdom to navigate this life, so that I may be a positive and Godly influence on my family and friends. Make me a better person. Refine the impurities in my heart. Father, I pray that You may increase in my life as I decrease. Thank you for hearing my prayer.

In Jesus' name,

Amen.

WHEN FACING UNCERTAIN TIMES

Jeremiah 17:7-8 (NKJV),
"Blessed is the man who trusts in the Lord,
and whose hope is the Lord. For he shall be
like a tree planted by the waters, which spreads
out its roots by the river, and will not fear
when heat comes; but its leaf will be green and
will not be anxious in the year of drought,
nor will cease from yielding fruit."

It's no secret that we are living in uncertain times. No one knows what tomorrow will bring. However, what is unknown to us is known by God. Uncertainty about the things here on this earth should not be a reason for any believer to become fearful. Of course, we have no idea what tomorrow, next week, or next month has in store for us. However, as believers who have been called to walk by faith and not by sight, we can have faith in the fact that Jesus Christ is alive and on His throne. We can have faith in the fact that He has numbered the hairs on our heads and before we were formed in our mother's womb, God already knew us. He knows our today, and He definitely knows our tomorrow.

Uncertainty can come in different forms. There can be financial, health-related, or relational uncertainty. It's during these times of uncertainty that it can be difficult to keep a positive outlook, because the unknown may seem bigger than anything else. Nonetheless, your faith should rest firmly on the Word of God and not on what your natural eyes can see. Your certainty should be in God's Word. Your certainty should be in God's promises.

One of the best passages of scriptures to crush the overwhelmingly fearful feelings that come with uncertainty is found in the book of Matthew 6:25-34 (ESV):

> 25 *"Therefore I tell you, do not be anxious about your life, what you will eat or what you will drink, nor about your body, what you will put on. Is not life more than food, and the body more than clothing?* 26 *Look at the birds of the air: they neither sow nor reap nor gather into barns, and yet your heavenly Father feeds them. Are you not of more value than they?* 27 *And which of you by being anxious can add a single hour to his span of life?* 28 *And why are you anxious about clothing? Consider the lilies of the field, how they grow: they neither toil nor spin,* 29 *yet I tell you, even Solomon in all his glory was not arrayed like one of these.* 30 *But if God so clothes the grass of the field, which today is alive and tomorrow is thrown into the oven, will he not much more clothe you, O you of little faith?* 31 *Therefore do not be anxious, saying, 'What shall we eat?' or 'What shall we drink?' or 'What shall we wear?'* 32 *For the Gentiles seek after all these things, and your heavenly Father knows that you need them all.* 33 *But seek first*

the kingdom of God and his righteousness, and all these things will be added to you. [34] *Therefore do not be anxious about tomorrow, for tomorrow will be anxious for itself. Sufficient for the day is its own trouble."*

PRAYER

Heavenly Father,

All glory belongs to You. All honour belongs to You. I am praying because I need You. I need Your love, and I need Your grace. I don't know what tomorrow holds for me. I don't know what it holds for my family. But Lord, I do know that You have said in Your Word that I should "be anxious for nothing," so I'm looking to You for direction. I am looking to You with eyes of faith for counsel, for provision, and for guidance. I refuse to lean on my own understanding, because when I look at things with my natural eyes, nothing makes any sense. However, I believe that there is a purpose greater than what my eyes can see. There is a reason why I am going through this trial, through this test. And if I must go through this test because it's Your will, I ask that You give me strength. Grant me the faith to stand firm and endure.

I pray that You stand by me, Lord Jesus. I don't know what I will face tomorrow, but I do know that Your Word tells me to submit to You, for You will make my paths straight. I know that Your Word in the book of Isaiah tells me that when I pass through the waters, You will be with me. When I pass through the rivers, they will not sweep over me. When I walk through the fire, I will not be burned, and the flames will not set me ablaze. In Your Word, I place my confidence for tomorrow. In Your Word, I place my hope and faith for tomorrow. You know the number of hairs on my head. You tell me not to fear because I am more valuable to You than many sparrows. I am grateful for Your word because it gives me confidence and strength when I am at my weakest.

Dear Lord, I ask that there be a hedge of protection around me, a hedge of protection around my family, my spouse, and my children. Place a hedge of protection around our health and around our home. I ask that the blood of Jesus Christ, the Risen King, cover my steps. You are a God who watches over me. You are faithful not to let my foot slip. You are a God who never sleeps nor slumbers. Victory belongs to You. Healing can only be found in You. Restoration comes only through You. My protection is under the blood of Jesus, the blood that never loses its power. I praise You and thank You for hearing my prayer.

Amen.

SECURED BY GOD

Matthew 6:33 (AMP),
"But first and most importantly seek
(aim at, strive after) His kingdom and His righteousness
[His way of doing and being right—
the attitude and character of God],
and all these things will be given to you also."

There are a few things that all people long for and need. We all need shelter. We all need food. We all long to be loved and to experience love. We all long for a sense of purpose, to feel like we are wanted and needed, whether through our families or careers.

Then there is a longing for a sense of security. Everything we want, need, and long for is linked to a sense of security in one aspect or another. If it's shelter, we want the security of knowing that we can afford that home or that apartment. If it's love, we want the security of loyalty and commitment. When it comes to our careers, we long for job security, or at least the security of a regular source of income.

Look closely at your life, and you will see that we all crave security. We are careful with our diet, because we want to secure our long-term health. We're diligent with our finances, because we want to secure our future. We are persistent with education, because we want to secure the best opportunities available. However, despite all our best efforts or how hard-working and diligent we may be, there are some storms that come into our lives which we are unable to prevent. Storms, challenges, and trials will come, and no amount of preparation can ever fully secure you for each storm, regardless of who you are, the size of your wallet, or your level of influence.

There is only One who offers refuge from every kind of storm that you could possibly face – Jesus Christ. It's only in Jesus that your future can be secure. It's only through the Son of God that you can secure eternal life. It's only in Jesus Christ that we can find a sense of security when it comes to our health, our finances, and our careers. Rather than seeking protection and refuge for yourself, seek Jesus Christ, and you will find protection and refuge in Him. When it comes to your health, its not enough to simply have a good diet and exercise regularly. You need to place your faith in Jesus Christ and He will preserve your health and well-being. It's only in the Lord that we can find real security. It's in Jesus Christ that we will be secure.

PRAYER

Lord Jesus,

You are ever faithful. You are my hiding place. In You, I am secure. Father, I ask for Your grace and protection over my life and my family. I believe that You are a God who knows the beginning and the end. You're a God who was, who is, and who will forever be. Although I do not know what the future may hold, I know that Psalm 37:25 (NKJV), says that "I have been young, and now am old; I have not seen the righteous forsaken, nor his descendants begging bread." You are a God who will never leave me, nor forsake me. You protect Your children.

I pray for supernatural protection, Lord. Your Word tells me that "You are a stronghold in the day of trouble." You are my refuge and my strength. You are the lion of the tribe of Judah.

Father there are many things that threaten us in this world and I ask for divine protection around myself and my family. I speak the blood of Jesus Christ to form a hedge of protection around over my life and my family. In You, I am secure. In Your presence, I am secured. And so, I invite You Master, into every area of my life.

Your Word says in Psalm 91:7 (NKJV): "A thousand may fall at your side, and ten thousand at your right hand; but it shall not come near you." I believe that no evil or darkness shall come near me because of You. You are the Most High God, the King of Kings, the Lord of Lords. My sense of security comes from Your Word.

Your Word says in Psalm 91:10-11 (NKJV), "[10] No evil shall befall you, nor shall any plague come near your dwelling; [11] For He shall give His angels charge over you, to keep you in all your ways."

I stand secure in faith of because of Your Word. No evil will befall me or my family. No plague will come near my home or my body, in the mighty name of Jesus Christ I pray. Even though I may not see with my eyes, I believe, as Your Word says, that angels are surrounding my family and me. You have charge over my life, Lord. You are a God who is faithful to deliver those who trust in Him. All my cares and worries I give to You, Lord. I surrender it all to You because You are the One who neither sleeps nor slumbers. Thank You for Your mercy. Thank You for Your grace. Thank You for hearing my prayer. I will trust in You and in Your Word.

Amen.

A PEACE BEYOND HUMAN UNDERSTANDING

When you draw closer to Jesus Christ, you will find Him to be a Wonderful Counsellor, a Mighty God, an Eternal Father, and the Prince of Peace, according to Isaiah 9:6. When you draw closer to the Lord, you will find Mark 10:27 to be true. You will see that with men things may be impossible, but not with God; with God all things are possible. So, be encouraged by God's Word. Don't allow the problem you're facing today to overwhelm you. Do not allow that burden to weigh you down. Don't allow the enemy to distract you. All that you need can be found in Christ.

May the peace of the Lord be upon your heart. May the peace offered by Jesus Christ envelope your life. May your eyes remain fixed on the perfect work that was done on the cross. May your faith stand on the solid rock that is Jesus Christ. May you find joy and triumph, victory and gladness as you chase the presence of God. May you find Him to be a certain God in the midst of an uncertain world.

As believers, when we are planted, anchored, and

immersed in Godly things, we then have access to the gift of peace that comes only through Jesus Christ. Should you open your heart and receive this gift, you will find that it's a peace with a cause. God's peace has an aim, and it brings about a result or an effect because you may see trouble, but the peace of the Lord will cause you not to be afraid. You will see a storm, but the Lord's peace will cause you not to be moved. Although you may walk through the valley of the shadow of death, the peace of God will cause you not to fear. The peace that we are given by Jesus Christ will undoubtedly have a positive effect on us. Therefore, we should desire to know Jesus Christ more intimately because only then will we know true and lasting peace.

PRAYER

Lord Jesus,

In John 14:27 (NKJV) You say, "Peace I leave with you, My peace I give to you; not as the world gives do I give to you. Let not your heart be troubled, neither let it be afraid." Give me peace, Lord, even when chaos and trouble surrounds me. Let my heart not be afraid for my God is a consuming fire. Let my heart not be afraid because greater is He who is in me than he who is in the world. When life is challenging and the enemy tries to hinder me, my soul will not be shaken because my God is a way maker. Father, may Your peace soothe my heart and spirit even as I pray right now.

If I come against anything that is not of God. If I come against anxiety, worry, stress, and fear. You have given me a spirit of power, and of love, and of a sound mind. I pray that Your heavenly spirit will infiltrate my mind, my home, and my heart. Your promise, God, is for peace that surpasses human understanding. I receive that promise. I pray that Your gentle and loving hand will open up my heart and give me an unshakcable peace. I pray that Your spirit will calm my heart. When my heart feels heavy, I pray that the Holy Spirit will be my comfort. When my life appears to be broken, Your Word and Your presence restores me. I declare peace over my life as I lay my burdens before You Lord. I declare that there is peace in my life because my life is in Your hands. I praise You for Your abundant mercy and grace that reigns over my entire life. I find peace in You, God, because when I am worn out, You renew my strength.

My Lord, I seek You because, in Your presence, there is a peace that can guard my mind and strengthen me. I do not lean on my own understanding, because You are an all-knowing God, so my trust is in You. Heal and remove everything that is troubling and unsettling in my life.

Father, when the storms of life seem endless and the enemy tries to steal my joy, I pray that you would calm my spirit. Let Your peace rule in my heart. Lord Jesus I believe and I receive Your promises for blessings of peace over my life. In the mighty name of Jesus Christ I pray.

Amen.

NO MORE FEAR

In the book of Proverbs, you'll come across a beautiful and comforting passage of scripture.

Proverbs 3:5-6 (ESV)
"⁵ Trust in the Lord with all your heart,
and do not lean on your own understanding.
⁶ In all your ways acknowledge him,
and he will make straight your paths."

Often, it's the things that you don't understand that make you fearful. Occasionally, there will be events, catastrophes, or incidents that happen in this world that we don't understand. Sometimes, we don't even understand the things happening to us individually. All this uncertainty and second-guessing can begin to open cracks in our armour for fear to creep into our lives. However, this is why we ought to fully trust in the Lord with all our heart. Leaning on our own understanding will only leave us with more questions than answers.

The Lord tells us in Isaiah 41:10 (NKJV), "Fear not, for I am with you; Be not dismayed, for I am your God. I will strengthen you, Yes, I will help you, I will uphold you with My righteous right hand." As believers, our lives should never be led by how we feel but rather by our faith in Jesus Christ. Our lives should not be crippled by worry, but instead our lives should be empowered and encouraged by the promises of God that tell us not to fear. This is not to say we won't ever experience the feelings of stress, anxiety, or even depression, because those things will come and try to attack us. However, these emotions and feelings will not overwhelm us. They will not take root and crush our faith because, as children of God, we are equipped through the Word of God to defeat these destructive feelings.

2 Timothy 1:7 (AMP) says, "For God did not give us a spirit of timidity or cowardice or fear, but [He has given us a spirit] of power and of love and of sound judgment and personal discipline [abilities that result in a calm, well-balanced mind and self-control]." So, be encouraged to stand against the spirit of fear through the authority that's in the name of Jesus Christ.

PRAYER

Father God,

I bow my head and lift my heart to You, a merciful and loving God. The only spirit I welcome and invite into my life, and into my home is the Spirit of God, the Holy Spirit. Come, Holy Spirit. Burn away any fear in my life. I pray for a holy fire that cleanses and removes all anxiety and uneasiness. Send a fire, Lord, that burns away everything that is not of You in my life.

The Bible states that You have not given me a spirit of fear but of power, love, and a sound mind. I declare, in the name of Jesus, that no spirit of fear will paralyse my thoughts and emotions. No spirit of fear will consume my heart or trouble me when I'm alone. I want the power of God to touch my life. Move in, Holy Spirit, and displace fear in my life. Move in my heart, Holy Spirit, and fill me with peace. My home will not be a fearful home. My heart will not be a fearful heart, because my trust and protection is in the God of Abraham, Isaac, and Jacob. Blessed be the name of the Lord.

Lord Jesus, I declare that I will not be crushed by my own worries and anxiety. I declare peace in my heart and mind. I look to You as the rock of my life, my fortress, my strong tower, and my strength. Break the chains of fear over my life. I will not be a slave to the spirit of fear any longer, because Your Word says whom the Son sets free is free indeed. I choose to trust in You King Jesus. Unto You I cast all worries, fears, and all of my burdens.

I find peace in Joshua 1:9 (NIV) which says, "Have I not commanded you? Be strong and courageous. Do not be afraid; do not be discouraged, for the Lord your God will be with you wherever you go." I declare that I will not be afraid. I will not fear because You are with me, the God of the universe, the Creator of the heavens and the earth. I am only strong and courageous because God is on my side. In Your Word, You say You have left peace with me. Your peace You have given to me and not as the world gives. I ask that You guide my thoughts and calm my fears. Let my heart not be troubled by this world. Lord, only Your presence can renew a fearful mind and I ask that you would help me not to be afraid.

Through the power that is in the blood of Jesus Christ, I will not allow fear to take control of my life. Help me to be confident in all situations, to stand assured knowing that You are in control. You hold the future in your hands, and I trust that everything will work together for my good. I ask that You deliver me and set me free from fear.

Take control Lord Jesus. Guide my thoughts. May Your peace invade and rule my heart. In Your presence, there is a quietness that is pure. My strength comes from You. Help me not to fear. Give me courage, Lord. Give me boldness. I don't want to be fearful in any area of my life. I choose to trust in You each day, each hour, each moment of my life. You gave Your life on the cross for me so that I may be set free and walk in victory.

As my heart desires to seek You, I know and trust that You are a God who is able to protect me from anything. You have not given me a spirit of fear, and I trust that You have removed every trace of fear from my life at this moment. I welcome Your power and Your love into my life. I will not fear because If God is for me, then who can be against me? Your love and care is endless, because You are a good Father. I thank You for hearing this prayer. In the mighty name of Jesus Christ I pray.

Amen.

DIVINE AND HEAVENLY PROTECTION

Isaiah 41:10 (ESV)
"Fear not, for I am with you;
be not dismayed, for I am your God;
I will strengthen you, I will help you,
I will uphold you with my righteous right hand."

Let's take a closer look at what this verse means. The first line is, "fear not, for I am with you." In other words, don't be alarmed or frightened. Don't be afraid. Don't be scared, because God is with you. Do you know what that means? We're not talking about armed security. We're not talking about the deadliest warriors on earth. We're talking about the creator of heaven and earth. Yahweh, Elohim is with you. He is a God who cannot be challenged. A God who is all powerful and all knowing.

The second line of Isaiah 41:10 is "be not dismayed, for I am your God." The Bible is telling us that there is no reason to be sorrowful. Don't wallow in worry. Don't wrestle with anxiety, because God Almighty has said, "I am your God." He is not limited in His ability, so why should you worry? He doesn't sleep nor does He slumber, so why should you be concerned about what walks in darkness? Do not be dismayed. Do not be distressed. God is with you.

The third line says, "I will strengthen you, I will help you." How privileged we are as children of the Most High God. The Father has not only told us not to fear or be dismayed, but He has also promised to strengthen us. So, should the devil attempt to point out your weaknesses, tell him that you are strong in the Lord. If your mind tries to tell you that you are limited or not strong enough, fight back with the Word of God. Remind yourself that God has said He will strengthen you. He will help you and come to your aid.

The final line says, "I will uphold you with my righteous right hand." To uphold is to support, sustain, preserve, and protect. It's in scriptures like these that we should find comfort and confidence in. We are protected by God Almighty, and there is no reason to fear.

PRAYER

Heavenly Father,

I thank You for Your goodness and Your mercy upon my life. I thank You, Lord, for being in my life! You are the Lord God Almighty, the great I Am. You are my refuge. You are the chief cornerstone. I choose to trust in You, the true and living God. You provide me with shelter from life's storms and difficulties.

I speak the blood of Jesus upon each and every member of my family for protection and preservation of life. I declare that the gates of hell shall not prevail against me or my loved ones. I plead the powerful blood of Jesus Christ upon the doorposts of my home. May Your blood cleanse every wall and room in my home Lord. I pray that a pillar of fire will surround and protect myself and my family and each and every night Father.

Lord, You have said You will not allow sickness and disease to come near me. I therefore declare that sickness and disease are far from me. I pray that You protect me and my family from everything we cannot see that tries to harm us. No demon from hell, no unclean spirit, no generational curses, no misfortune will touch my family because of You, Lord Jesus.

I pray that You will protect me and my loved ones. Sustain us Lord and preserve us always. I call on the name of Jesus Christ, the name that was given power above all names. I trust that You will protect me from the terror by night and the arrow that flies by day. I receive that promise, and I believe that You are faithful to Your Word Lord.

Amen.

PUT GOD FIRST

Dear Christian, since you are a follower of Jesus Christ, since you are a believer, are you striving to be more and more like Jesus Christ each and every day?

James 1:22-25 (AMP) says, "[22]* But prove yourselves doers of the word [actively and continually obeying God's precepts], and not merely listeners [who hear the word but fail to internalize its meaning], deluding yourselves [by unsound reasoning contrary to the truth].* [23]* For if anyone only listens to the word without obeying it, he is like a man who looks very carefully at his natural face in a mirror;* [24]* for once he has looked at himself and gone away, he immediately forgets what he looked like.* [25]* But he who looks carefully into the perfect law, the law of liberty, and faithfully abides by it, not having become a [careless] listener who forgets but an active doer [who obeys], he will be blessed and favored by God in what he does [in his life of obedience]."*

If you confess that you are saved, does your life reflect that? If you confess that you have faith in God, do your actions reflect that? Do you truly walk by faith and not by sight?

Dear Christian, since you are a follower of Jesus Christ, are you following the example that the Lord set while He was here on earth? Are you praying often? Are you taking time away from the noise and distractions of the world to spend time alone with God? Are you praying and fasting? Are you doing what Christ did? These are necessary and important questions for all of us to ask ourselves from time to time. Are we following the example set before us by Jesus Christ? Are we removing ourselves from the busyness of life so that we can pray? Are we turning off the distractions of the world so that we can pray? If the answer is no, then I encourage you to start today.

Start praying today. Start making your spiritual life a priority today. Start following Jesus Christ's example today. Begin to make a concentrated effort when it comes to spending time in God's Word. Become consistent in your walk with Christ. Become relentless as you search for a deeper level of fellowship with God. Start today!

PRAYER

Heavenly Father,

I come to You seeking refuge and protection. I come to You in recognition of Your great might and power. I worship Your holy name, Lord. I adore You, Lord Jesus. I thank You for Your wonderful sacrifice. Your precious blood has cleansed me of the filthy rags of sin, and Your mercy has clothed me in a robe of righteousness, a robe that covers me from head to toe, all because of the perfect work You completed on the cross.

Lord Jesus, help me to shun all of the distractions in this world. Give me a heart and a mind filled with wisdom and understanding so that I can realise that I have so much more to gain in you than in this world. I pray that my life would be a reflection of Your grace and mercy. I pray that my life would be a testimony so that others can see how You can change a person and use them for Your glory. Lord, I pray that my character would be a reflection of the wonderful and transformative work that You can do in the hearts of sinners. Father, protect me from the busyness of this world. Help me not to be attached to the temporary things in this world.

I surrender my life and my loved ones into Your caring hands. You are a God full of compassion. I pray for Your hand of protection upon me and my family. Encompass us, Lord God Almighty, with a heavenly wall of fire. Surround me and my family with Your hedge of protection. Your blood, Lord Jesus, is living and it is powerful. You are my shield and defence. Your Word is a lamp unto my feet and a light unto my path. Do not let me stumble, King Jesus. I open my heart and my life to You so that You may take priority. I pray that You will overthrow the plans and the plots of my enemies.

Help me to overcome, in the name of Jesus. Fight my battles, Lord, as You have promised in Your Word. Your Word says in Exodus 14:14 (NKJV) that "The

Lord will fight for you, and you shall hold your peace." I pray that You will defend my family and I, and help us to hold our peace. I pray that we are going to stand still to see the hand of God move in our lives, in the name of Jesus Christ.

You are a God who moves mountains, and regardless of the things happening around me, regardless of the things going on in this world, You are our protector, our keeper, and our Redeemer. Regardless of what may come, You are still on Your throne. You are still a good God who will never leave me nor forsake me. You are a God who brings peace in troubling times.

I pray that the Holy Spirit will help me to prioritise You, King Jesus. You are the King of my heart, You are the Lord who rules and reigns in my life, and You are number one.

Lord, for my life, take all the glory. For my family and children, take all the glory. For my health, take all the glory Lord. For all that I am, take all the glory. I bless Your precious name for listening to my prayer.

In Jesus' name I pray,

Amen.

GOD WILL MAKE A WAY

Humans love to be able to measure. We love predictable outcomes. But life doesn't always work that way. Our earthly logic doesn't apply to every situation. In our minds, victory in life is all about our capability, our credentials, and our material things. We believe that unless we look impressive to the rest of the world, we have no chance of succeeding in life. But God has the power to override all of that. God doesn't look for the strongest among us to demonstrate His power. That would be too simple, too predictable. If God were to only use the strongest among us then we could essentially rationalise the Lord and rob him of his glory. If God were to only use the strongest among us to do his work, many of us would take God out of the equation and say "well that person was always an outstanding and gifted individual."

The Bible says in 1 Corinthians 1:27 (ESV), "But God chose what is foolish in the world to shame the wise; God chose what is weak in the world to shame the strong." This means you can't predict how God will move or act. What we deem to be foolish, God will use to shame the wise. What we deem to be weak, God will use to shame the strong. His ways are not like our ways.

Your biggest challenge can be used by the Lord to usher in your biggest breakthrough and blessing. Ask Joseph. The worst thing that could have happened to him, being betrayed by his own brothers, turned out to be the very thing that catapulted him into his God-ordained destiny. Ask the woman with the issue of blood. The disease that had taken so much from her, a disease that robbed her of her friends, her wealth, and dignity, that same disease is what led her to experience the miraculous healing power of the Master. Our weaknesses can often be the cause of us experiencing the power of God.

We should be encouraged by the Word of the Lord which says in Romans 8:28 (NKJV), "And we know that all things work together for good to those who love God, to those who are the called according to His purpose." Trials and problems will come. At one point or another, we'll be forced to fight battles that we'd rather not. We'll come across challenges that we may not want to face. However, we have a saviour in Jesus Christ. We have a miracle working God and He will make a way when there seems to be no way. God has promised us in His Word that all things will work together for our good if we love him. That means that the pain and disappointment you feel now will work together for your good. The betrayal and hurt you feel now will work together for your good. Be encouraged, you may not see it now, it may not make sense right now. However, trust the Lord to lead you. Trust Him to make you lie down in green pastures. Trust Him to lead you to still waters. Trust God to make a way when there seems to be no way because ultimately, He is in control and your life is in His loving hands.

PRAYER

Heavenly Father,

Your Word says in Jeremiah 33:3 (NKJV), "Call to me, and I will answer you, and show you great and mighty things, which you do not know." I pray that You will show me great and mighty things. Do a mighty work in my life, Lord. Show me great and mighty things, O God. Whatever I may need, whichever area that needs divine intervention my life Lord, I invite you to step in. Break every chain that's stopping me from progressing or advancing forward. Break every chain in my relationships, marriage, career, and health. Loosen those chains just as You did with Paul and Silas. You have said that You are near to all who call on You in truth.

Increase my faith so that I may know Your power. Give me a breakthrough Father. At Your name, mountains move. At Your name, storms become calm. Lord Jesus, creation sings with joy. At the sound of Your name, demons flee. At the name of Jesus Christ, walls and barriers come down. Not only will every knee bow and every tongue confess that You are Lord, but every stronghold and every force of darkness will be defeated in the mighty name of Jesus Christ, I pray.

There is no power greater than You. Nothing standing against me can prosper so long as You are my God. Help me to trust in Your power when I face difficult situations that seem to have no solution. You have promised that those who seek the Lord lack no good thing. Let me lack nothing as I look to You for every need and desire in my life. Wipe out everything oppressive and everything depressive in my life. Lord I declare a complete breakthrough in every area of my life, for I am victorious through Christ Jesus. I come against every form of worry in my life. Lord even if things seem to be impossible, I trust and believe that with God all things are possible.

I pray that the Holy Spirit will guide and direct me. May He help me to make wise decisions and lead me to walk in Your will. Lord, make a way for me where there seems to be no way. Give me hope where there seems to be no hope. Lord I pray that You will present possibilities in the middle of impossible situations.

I lift up my faith and place my confidence in You so that I will be victorious, in the mighty name of Jesus. Father, surely goodness and mercy will follow me all the days of my life. I am grateful to You because I have the power, through the blood of Jesus Christ, to overcome daily. Direct my steps and fulfil Your plans for my life. Let my feet run swiftly to follow after You. Help me to fix my eyes on You Jesus. I pray for a supernatural breakthrough. May I begin to see Your power at work in my life. May the Holy Spirit open my eyes so that I can see Your goodness daily.

In Jesus' name I pray,

Amen.

GOD'S MERCY

We all need the mercy of God in our lives. It was God's mercy that woke us up this morning. It's through His mercy and grace that we are protected. It's through His mercy and grace that we can find healing, and peace, and provision. Don't take the Lord's mercy for granted. We are all undeserving of His love and forgiveness. However, He still freely loves and forgives us when we turn away from our corrupt ways.

In 2 Chronicles 30:9 (NIV), the scripture says, "If you return to the Lord, then your fellow Israelites and your children will be shown compassion by their captors and will return to this land, for the Lord your God is gracious and compassionate. He will not turn his face from you if you return to him."

Now in your own life, If you've backslidden, come back to Jesus. If you've sinned, repent and come back to Jesus. If you've placed your trust elsewhere, come back to Jesus. It's important for us, as believers, to remain rooted in the Lord. We need to be calling out for His hand to touch our lives. We need to be crying out for His love, grace, and tender mercy to fill our lives. We need to repent and turn to the Lord.

God, in His sovereignty and compassion, gives us gifts and blessings that we don't deserve. We don't deserve eternal life, but He offers it to us. We don't deserve unconditional love, but He offers it to us. We don't deserve His amazing grace, but He gives it to us! Be encouraged that if you call on the Lord, He will hear you and He will see you. He loves those who feel unloved. He wants those who feel lonely and rejected to find fullness and belonging in Him. For those who are filled with shame and feel condemned, repent and return to Jesus Christ, because He will wash away all your sins. Be encouraged and know that there is no condemnation or shame when you're in the Lord. Hold on to Isaiah 43:25 (ESV) that says, "I, I am he who blots out your transgressions for my own sake, and I will not remember your sins."

PRAYER

Dear Lord Jesus,

I ask for Your mercy and forgiveness. Your Word says in Hebrews 4:16 (NIV), "Let us then approach God's throne of grace with confidence, so that we may receive mercy and find grace to help us in our time of need." This is my time of need. I acknowledge You to be the one true God, the ruler of the universe. I bow before You, King Jesus, and say You are Lord of Lords. You are great and mighty, but You are also filled with affection and compassion. You are a consuming fire, but You are also absolute in Your love.

While I was still a sinner, You died for me, Lord Jesus. I repent of my sins. I repent for the sins that I have committed in mind and in action. Have mercy on me, Lord. In Your love, there is no fear. Your perfect love expels all fear. Your Word says in Lamentations 3:22-23 (ESV), "The steadfast love of the Lord never ceases; his mercies never come to an end; they are new every morning; great is your faithfulness."

Thank You for new mercies every day. Today's mercies are more than enough for today's troubles. Thank You for your unending love. Even when I walk away from You, Lord, and fall short, You still love me. You still open Your arms in love. You still call me to repent and to come back to You. Your love is strong and steadfast. Your love is what protects me from the enemy. Your love has protected me from battles seen and unseen. Your love has blocked attacks from the enemy that I did not see.

Your grace continues to sustain me. Your divine mercy always sees me as I truly am, yet You still care for me and love me constantly. I offer thanksgiving to You, Lord. Thank You. Thank You for Your Son, Jesus Christ, who rescued me from sin. So strong was Your love that You would not allow even sin to separate us. Instead of eternal death, You offered eternal life. John 3:16 (NKJV) says, "For God so loved the world that He gave His only begotten Son, that whoever believes in Him should not perish but have everlasting life." Thank You for Your mercy, Lord Jesus.

You laid aside Your glory, came to earth as a man, and suffered and died for me so that I might be freed from the clutches of the enemy. You came to set me free, free from every garment of shame, death, sin, and unrighteousness. You clothed me with love and mercy. You have clothed me with joy everlasting.

I bless Your holy name because You are a covenant-keeping God. I trust and depend on You, Lord. Have mercy on me, O God. When the enemy tries to attack me, when he sends calamity and disaster my way, I pray that You will be my protector Lord Jesus. Help me to stand firm and know that You are my stronghold in the day of trouble. You are the rock of my salvation. The Lord is my rock, my fortress, and my deliverer. My God, You are my strength. You are my shield, the horn of my salvation, and my stronghold. You see my struggles, Lord. You see my pain and I cry out to you. Help me King Jesus when the challenges of life are overwhelming, when the trials of life are too hard for me. Lord, let Your mercy be shown.

I trust You to be my help and comfort always. You see my needs. You see the areas I lack. You are a God who provides. I declare that Your goodness and mercies shall never depart from me, in Jesus' name. Your Word says in Psalm 145:9 (NKJV) that "The Lord is good to all, and His tender mercies are over all His works." You are rich in mercy. Help me not to rely on my own strength. Thank You for always welcoming me in my weakness, in my brokenness, and in my desperation.

Thank You for never turning away from me, nor turning a deaf ear to me. You are the fountain of kindness and the giver of grace upon grace. Give me the courage and strength to overcome the enemy. You have promised to always stand by me. Thank You for hearing my prayer and may you continue to grant me blessings and mercy.

In Jesus' name I pray,

Amen.

STRONG FAITH

Faith is believing that God will honour and execute His Word in your hour of need. To have faith is to trust in the Almighty God and believe that He will come through for you in all circumstances. Faith becomes more defined, refined, and strengthened in difficult circumstances. However, this is no reason to be fearful, because you don't need faith the size of Noah's ark.

In His teaching on faith, Jesus requires us to have faith as small as a mustard seed. In Matthew 17:20 (ESV), "He said to them, 'Because of your little faith. For truly, I say to you, if you have faith like a grain of mustard seed, you will say to this mountain, "Move from here to there," and it will move, and nothing will be impossible for you.' " If you feel like your faith is inadequate, then remember these two things: your only requirement is to have faith the size of a mustard seed and to look to Jesus Christ in all situations. It takes faith to receive Jesus Christ as your Lord and saviour, and so each one of us has a measure of faith to begin with. The growth or increase in faith, however, is a personal responsibility. Romans 10:17 (NKJV) says, "So then faith comes by hearing, and hearing by the word of God." The food that feeds faith is the Word of God, so in the midst of whatever you are going through, the Word of God will strengthen your faith regardless of how deep the waters are or how big the giant is.

1 John 5:5 (AMP) reads, "Who is the one who is victorious and overcomes the world? It is the one who believes and recognizes the fact that Jesus is the Son of God." So be encouraged by the Word of the Lord and have faith in the One who speaks and the wind obeys. Have faith in the One who speaks and creates. Have faith in the One whose breath has eternal life. Have faith in the One who has broken the grip of death. Have faith in Jesus Christ.

PRAYER

Dear Lord,

You say in Your Word in Isaiah 41:10 (NKJV), "Fear not, for I am with you; be not dismayed, for I am your God. I will strengthen you, yes, I will help you, I will uphold you with My righteous right hand." Thank you Lord because You have provided such a beautiful and comforting assurance for me. At times, when l am attacked by doubts and the spirit of fear from the enemy, help me to have faith. Your Word is a present reminder that You are with me and you are in control. Your Word reassures and guides me, especially in moments when my faith is tested. For this, I am grateful.

I bow before You today. I set my heart in Your hands. I humbly ask for Your presence to surround me. Lord my hope is in You because You have promised me in Your Word that You will strengthen me and help me, You will uphold me with Your righteous right hand.

Father, I am seeking an increase of faith to sustain me along life's journey. I acknowledge You, Lord Jesus, as my personal Saviour. I acknowledge that You are the way, the truth, and the life. I know that You are God. I know that You are all-powerful. I know that You are in control.

When my faith is weak, O Lord, give me strength. I pray that I would draw strength from Your Word. May Your joy give me strength. I commit myself and my desires to You. Help me never to forget to whom I belong to. As soon as I encounter a challenge or feel overwhelmed, I pray that the Holy Spirit would remind me that I have victory in Jesus Christ.

Heavenly Father, strengthen my faith today. Matthew 17:20 (NKJV) says, "So Jesus said to them, 'Because of your unbelief; for assuredly, I say to you, if you have faith as a mustard seed, you will say to this mountain, 'Move from here to there,' and it will move; and nothing will be impossible for you.'" Strengthen my faith Lord. Give me the kind of faith that not only changes my life but the lives of those closest to me.

As I face the mountains of life in different shapes and sizes, I believe in the promise of Your Word. I pray that I might have the kind of faith that can move mountains. The mountains of doubt in my life or the mountains of sinful, generational cycles. Whatever it is that is hindering me, Lord, build my faith, strengthen my faith, so that I can walk in victory.

Father God, I pray that you will enable me to have the kind of faith that looks beyond my problems and sees that there is victory and triumph in Christ. I pray that my reality may be Your Word, God. Help me to walk by faith and not by sight. When Job lost everything, he was able to say in Job 13:15 (KJV), "Though he slay me, yet will I trust in him…" Mighty God, this is the level of faith that I want, the type of faith that understands that even in pain and sorrow, You are still in control and Your love for me is still great.

Help me, Lord, so that I can be able to live by faith and please You. Despite the temptation to give up and to surrender to my weaknesses, remind me that You are the Way, the Truth and the Life.

When Daniel was confronted with the threat of the lions, he had true faith in Your power. You acted on his faith in You, and Daniel was unharmed. You are the same mighty and powerful God who can deliver me from my own den of lions. I commit my ways to You. Empower me to stand in faith and face the lions before me.

Your Word in 1 John 4:4 (NKJV) assures me when it says, "You are of God, little children, and have overcome them, because He who is in you is greater than he who is in the world." I declare this to be true in my life, in Jesus's name. Greater is He that is in me than he who is in the world. I believe and accept that I am Your child. You will never leave me nor forsake me. No matter how overwhelming my trials may seem, You are greater and more powerful than anything.

Lord, I want to live for You. I want to live a life of faith because without faith, it is impossible to please You. So I ask that You would strengthen my faith in You. Please help me to fearlessly put my trust in You. Thank You for hearing my prayer.

In Jesus' name,

Amen.

HE STILL HEALS TODAY

Hebrews 13:8 (NKJV) says,
"Jesus Christ is the same yesterday, today, and forever."

This is an important scripture for every believer to remember. Our Lord Jesus Christ does not change. The same Jesus who cast out spirits with His Word and healed the sick, according to Matthew 8:16, is still the same Jesus who can heal and set people free today! He can still heal those who are broken-hearted, just as well as He can heal the blind today.

Matthew 14:35-36 (NKJV) tells us, "And when the men of that place recognized Him, they sent out into all that surrounding region, brought to Him all who were sick, and begged Him that they might only touch the hem of His garment. And as many as touched it were made perfectly well." We can still touch the hem of His garment through faith. We can still be made perfectly well because the Word of God in Mark 9:23 (NKJV) tells us, "If you can believe, all things are possible to him who believes." Jesus Christ is the same yesterday, today, and forevermore. His miraculous power has not faded. His ability to restore, to mend, and to make you whole again has not diminished. The wonder-working power in His blood still operates today.

At times, the Lord allows us to go through certain things so that His power can be demonstrated. On other occasions, He allows us to face certain trials so that our faith may be strengthened and for our character to develop. There are also times where His healing may not be what we expect in the sense that you can have physical pain yet still see the goodness of God. You can experience a physical trial, but the Lord will bless you with grace and peace so that you may be a living testimony to encourage others. The Lord's will is what will always prevail.

Matthew 15:30 (NKJV) reads, "Then great multitudes came to Him, having with them the lame, blind, mute, maimed, and many others; and they laid them down at Jesus' feet, and He healed them." The same Jesus who healed great multitudes hundreds of years ago can still heal you today. The same Jesus who healed blind Bartimaeus and the woman with the issue of blood is still healing today. Lay down your requests at the feet of the Father, and believe that He can do a wonderful and miraculous work in you and for you, even now.

PRAYER

Dear Heavenly Father,

I come before You today seeking a touch from Your almighty hand. Do Your will, Father, and have Your way in my life. You are the King of Kings and Lord of Lords. There is none like You. There is no other healer besides You. There is no better doctor than You, King Jesus.

Your Word in Isaiah 53:5 (NKJV) says, "But He was wounded for our transgressions, He was bruised for our iniquities; The chastisement for our peace was upon Him, And by His stripes we are healed." I declare healing in my life, and I believe that I am healed emotionally, physically, and mentally in Jesus' name. This is not because I say so, but it is because Your Word says so. I have faith that it can happen if it is in Your will that it should happen, Lord. You know what is best for me, Father. If it is Your will that I may not be healed yet, then I believe You will give me the grace to overcome. You will give me the strength to endure.

Lord, so long as You are with me as my shepherd, as my guide, then I know that even though I walk through the valley of the shadow of death, I will fear no evil, for Your rod and staff will comfort me. I pray that I may not be discouraged or afraid, even if my healing doesn't come within my own timing. I will choose to trust Your timing above mine. I choose to have faith in Your divine plan because my life is in Your loving hands. My future and my health are all in Your hands, regardless of what earthly doctors may say. I am always confident in You. I am always safe and taken care of because I know the greatest healer. I will not chase healing, but instead, I will chase You, Lord Jesus. I will not chase miracles, but I will chase the One who performs miracles.

Because of the price You paid for me on the cross, I know that I can always count on You, King Jesus, even in times when it doesn't feel like You are there. Your Word says You are the same yesterday, today, and forever. I can always depend on You to never change. I can always depend on Your love to see me through and to never cease. I depend on You in all things, at all times, and in all ways. Though the world changes, circumstances change, people change, and I change, You, Lord Jesus, never change. You were a healer many years ago, and You are a healer today. You were a miracle worker many years ago, and You are a miracle worker today. I believe that I can always count on You, my Father.

Thank You for hearing this prayer. I receive healing in Your presence. I receive restoration in Your presence. I am made whole again in Your presence. I bless Your holy name.

Amen.

THE PRESENCE OF GOD

In this life, we come into the presence of many things and many people. The type of atmosphere we encounter, or rather the atmosphere created by the people we're surrounded with, can do one of two things: they can take us into the presence of God, or they can push us away from His presence.

Moses is someone who reached a point where he knew and understood what the Lord's presence meant.

Exodus 33:14-15 (NKJV) says, [14] "And He said, 'My Presence will go with you, and I will give you rest.' [15] Then he said to Him, 'If Your Presence does not go with us, do not bring us up from here.'" Moses realized the significance of God's presence. Without it, there was no power, no peace or joy, so Moses declared to God that he would not go anywhere without the Lord's presence.

Exodus 33:16 (NKJV) reads, "For how then will it be known that Your people and I have found grace in Your sight, except You go with us? So we shall be separate, Your people and I, from all the people who are upon the face of the earth." This verse tells us that there is grace in the presence of God. There is something unique and distinctive that can only be found in God's presence. Something so transformative and divine that it will separate you from everyone else in the world. We should all have the desire to encounter the presence of God at some point in our lives, an encounter that will revive and refresh us.

Acts 2:17 (NKJV) says, "And it shall come to pass in the last days, says God, That I will pour out of My Spirit on all flesh; Your sons and your daughters shall prophesy, Your young men shall see visions, Your old men shall dream dreams." God has promised to pour out His spirit on all flesh in the last days. Our cry and desire should be that we are not left out of this outpouring promised in the Bible. Make sure your heart is not hardened to the presence of God. Make sure your schedule is not so busy that you miss your divine appointment with God in your prayer closet.

Blind Bartimaeus refused to let Jesus just pass him by. In Mark 10:47 (NKJV) the Bible says, "And when he heard that it was Jesus of Nazareth, he began to cry out and say, 'Jesus, Son of David, have mercy on me!' " We too must have that same attitude. We need to be crying out to the Lord, "Don't pass by without pouring out Your spirit over my life, over my home, and over my family. Pass me not, O gentle Saviour!"

PRAYER

King Jesus,

The Alpha and Omega, You have saved me in every way possible. You have made me complete in Your love and mercy. There is no one comparable to You and for this reason, I bow and submit to You. I bow down and confess that You are Lord. I need You in my life. Pass me not, my Saviour. I need just a touch for my life to be blessed, for my situation to turn around. Just a touch of the hem of Your garment, and my entire family can be restored, my health can be restored, and my faith can be strengthened. I praise you because You are a wonder working God, and I come seeking Your presence today.

Just as Moses declared, if Your presence does not go with me, then I will not move. I pray for a mighty visitation from You, Lord Jesus. Let Your presence be known in my home. Lord, may You surround me. I will hold on to Exodus 33:14 (NKJV) and confess this verse in my life. You have said in Your Word, "My Presence will go with you, and I will give you rest." Lead me, and I will follow. Go ahead of me and be with me always, so that I may walk in communion with You. I pray that nothing will push me away from Your presence.

May You order my steps in everything I do, everywhere I go, and wherever I am. Guide and lead me, for You are my shepherd. Psalm 23:3 (NKJV) says, "He restores my soul; He leads me in the paths of righteousness for His name's sake." I pray that You will order my each and every step so that I may walk in a manner that is pleasing to You.

May the Holy Spirit be real to me. May He help me to focus on things that are pure, true, and right. Help me to be slow to anger. Help me to be forgiving. Help me to have a sweet and peaceful spirit that will reflect You and the work You are doing in me.

Be a light unto my path, King Jesus. Eradicate any evil in my life and expose every trap set by the enemy. I pray that You may grant me wisdom and peace today. May the joy of the Lord shine through me, the joy spoken of in Philippians 4:4 (NKJV), "Rejoice in the Lord always. Again I will say, rejoice!" I rejoice in all of Your goodness and faithfulness.

I rejoice in You, Lord, because your Word says in Philippians 4:6-7 (NKJV), "⁶ Be anxious for nothing, but in everything by prayer and supplication, with thanksgiving, let your requests be made known to God; ⁷ and the peace of God, which surpasses all understanding, will guard your hearts and minds through Christ Jesus." I pray that Your peace will guard my heart and mind. Even though I don't know every step of Your plan, I do know and trust that Your plan will be for my good.

Your Word says in Jeremiah 29:11-13 (NIV), "¹¹ For I know the plans I have for you," declares the Lord, "plans to prosper you and not to harm you, plans to give you hope and a future. ¹² Then you will call on me and come and pray to me, and I will listen to you. [13] You will seek me and find me when you seek me with all your heart.' ”

I thank You for Your promise that when I call on You, You will listen. Thank You for Your promise that when I seek You, with all of my heart, I will find You. Help me to be vigilant, Holy Spirit, so that I will not be found around ungodly friends or associates who may push me away from God. Holy Ghost, do not to allow my feet to walk in the same path as sinners. Instead, I pray that You will place me in good company, around people who love the Lord and people who will encourage me in faith. Birth within me a hunger and thirst to seek after Your presence Lord. Give me the right attitude to pursue You patiently. Hold me and guide me, Lord. May Your love surround me and may I always be found hidden in Your presence.

In Jesus' mighty name I pray,

Amen.

PRAISE THE LORD

You can get to know God through His Word and through personal experience. The Bible tells us in John 1:1 (ESV), "In the beginning was the Word, and the Word was with God, and the Word was God." As believers, we can be assured that the more we meditate on the Word, the more God is revealed to us. James 4:8 (ESV) says, "Draw near to God, and he will draw near to you. Cleanse your hands, you sinners, and purify your hearts, you double-minded." The Bible essentially tells us that as we get closer to God and draw near to him with a contrite, repentant heart, then he will draw near to us.

One of the ways you can draw closer to the Lord is to always have a heart full of praise. When you make praise a habit, you are continuously demonstrating that God is first in your life. It's all about Him. It's all about His glory. It's all about His goodness. Your focus and attention is always on the Lord when you make it a practice to praise Him daily.

There are many reasons to praise the Lord. We can praise Him for His protection, for His mercy, His grace and most definitely, His love. The love of God is divine, true, and everlasting. The Bible goes as far as stating that God is love! So great is His love that John 3:16 (NKJV) says, "For God so loved the world that He gave His only begotten Son, that whoever believes in Him should not perish but have everlasting life." The love of our almighty God, Jehovah, is characterized by grace, forgiveness, and mercy. His divine love is eternal and unconditional! May you recognize the love of the Lord over your life, a love that always protects you, a love that always provides for you, a love that forgives you.

Our God is worthy to be praised and adored. Praise Him for His consistency. His love is steadfast, unmovable, and never changing. Even when we are incapable of living consistently in a manner that is pleasing to Him, He is still loving and righteous. We all have to acknowledge our own inconsistencies when it comes to living righteously, because we are all sinners by nature. This means we must always seek the mercy of God. We must repent from our sins, and we must also praise Him and give Him thanks for His goodness, for simply loving and caring for us daily, even through our own inconsistencies. We must praise and thank Him, because we are truly blessed that His love is unending and it never changes.

PRAYER

Dear Father,

You are the king of my heart. You are my Saviour, Lord Jesus. Out of love, You came to this earth and You were crucified on a cross so that I may be saved. I praise You for such a deep, supernatural love that I could never repay. How great is Your love, God Almighty, that You gave Your only begotten Son that I should not perish but have everlasting life. I did nothing to deserve this, yet You freely gave Your Son so that I may be saved. I praise you for such an amazing love.

I thank You for Your Word that tells me in Jeremiah 1:5 (NKJV), "Before I formed you in the womb I knew you; before you were born I sanctified you..." May Your name always be praised for such love. I thank You for meeting my greatest need, which is to be loved unconditionally. Thank you for a love that calls me to repentance. You know all and see all, all that is done in the light and all deeds and thoughts in the darkness. And regardless of knowing my most shameful secrets, You still decided to offer me a perfect, sacrificial, and eternal love. You offered me grace and mercy, despite my faults. You showed me a powerful love.

Whenever I have needed You, You have been there for me. Whenever I have called on Your name, You have heard my cry. I am grateful for Your love, mercy, and grace, though I do not deserve it. Thank You for Your faithfulness even through tough times. To You alone be the glory.

You are the God of grace, the One who knows my thoughts and feelings, the One who sees my deepest desires. Lord, You understand my weariness and hear my cries. I am grateful to be able to call on Your name. It is a privilege to be saved, loved, and cared for by You. May You walk beside me every day, Lord Jesus.

You are a constant friend. May Your presence surround my home and stay with me all always. Only in You do I place my belief and confidence for all things, because You have proven Yourself time and time again to be a God I can depend on.

I pray that a divine and holy peace, just like a river, may overflow in my soul. I pray, Holy Spirit, that You will always remain with me, and may I never forget that. Help me to trust more and worry less, to have more faith and no fear, to have more belief and no doubt. Help me to know the Lord better. Help me to know His Word and promises for my life. I pray that You, Holy Ghost, will help me to put Jesus Christ first in every area of my life.

Lord Jesus, I pray for the grace to live one day at a time and rejoice in each new day. Help me to not worry about tomorrow but instead focus on what You're doing right now. I place my trust in Your promises. I trust that You will take care of all my burdens. You, Lord, can meet every one of my needs. You are worthy to be exalted, and I lift Your name on high, Father. All the glory be unto You.

In Jesus' name I pray,

Amen.

GODLY PASSIONS AND DESIRES

Quite often people ask the question, "If Jesus walked on the earth today, what would He do? Would he approve of some of the churches of today? Would he approve of how many professing Christians live their day-to-day lives?" However, the better question to ask is, "What did Jesus do when on this earth? What example did Jesus give us when it comes to how a Christian should live their life?"

If you look at the life of Our Lord while on earth, He prayed. He prayed often, and He prayed consistently. He prayed early in the morning, late at night, and even all through the night. Luke 5:16 (NKJV) says it all: "So He Himself often withdrew into the wilderness and prayed." It wasn't just a single occasion that He withdrew and went to pray. Jesus often withdrew so that He could spend quality time in prayer.

We must ask ourselves:

Am I following the example set by Jesus Christ?

Am I removing myself from the busyness of life so that I can pray?

Am I turning off the distractions of the world so that I can pray?

Am I following the example of Jesus Christ who prayed often and consistently?

If you answered "no" to any of those questions, you can start today. Make the change in your prayer life today and seek the Lord's face for yourself. Seek Him for guidance, for wisdom, and for direction. Seek Him first each and every day. Our hearts' cry should be that the Holy Spirit will stir up Godly passions and desires within us. Colossians 3:2 (KJV) says, "Set your affection on things above, not on things on the earth." You only show affection to someone or something you are passionate about. With this understanding, our aspiration should be to have strong Godly desires. We need a desire and a passion for prayer, a desire and a passion for the Word of God, a desire and a passion for witnessing to lost souls. A desire and a passion to seek the Lord wholeheartedly.

PRAYER

Lord Jesus,

My heart is bowed before You today. I stand in awe of Your power. I ask that You wash my sins away, as I look to You as my refuge and strength. I look to You as an ever-present help throughout my life. Lord I pray that You will look within me. Assess my heart and examine my passions. Should You find anything that is not pleasing, I ask that You remove it. May the Holy Spirit help me to cultivate Godly desires in my life. As I strive to set my mind on You, help me to remain focused on heavenly things, not on earthly things which have only temporal value.

Psalm 16:8 (NKJV) says, "I have set the Lord always before me: because he is at my right hand, I shall not be moved." God, I pray that I may always set You before me. I ask for the Holy Spirit to always convict me to put You first, King Jesus, in all my ways. Help me to pray often and consistently. Holy Spirit, help me to pray earnestly with boldness and faith. I know that through prayer I can gain spiritual victory. Only through prayer can I develop a more meaningful and deeper relationship with You, Lord, so I come to You today in need of Your grace and forgiveness. I repent for every ungodly desire and passion that I have entertained in my life. I am in need of Your mercy Lord, and I ask that You help me in all my ways.

Help me, Holy Spirit, to set the Lord before me. I desire to live the life spoken of in Proverbs 1:7 (NIV) which says, "The fear of the Lord is the beginning of knowledge, but fools despise wisdom and instruction." I pray that I may have the fear of the Lord in my heart. I desire to live a life where You are the biggest love of my heart Lord Jesus. Let me find joy and delight in nothing else but in the things of God. Give me a strong and passionate desire to serve You with all my heart and soul. Your Word in Deuteronomy 10:21 (NKJV) tells me, "He is your praise, and He is your God, who has done for you these great and awesome things which your eyes have seen." You are the only one who deserves the praises of my heart because of Your perfection and holiness.

Thank you for hearing my prayer, Lord Jesus.

Amen.

STRENGTH FROM ABOVE

Sometimes in life we encounter pain. We encounter heartache, and we can face circumstances that can cause us to ask questions. There are some situations that simply drain our energy and strength. As believers, we need to realize that we cannot overcome everything that comes our way without the help of the Lord. Without falling into the arms of the Father, the pain will always be too much. Without the strength and comfort of the Holy Spirit, heartache will destroy us. Without the hope, faith, and knowledge of knowing that Jesus Christ defeated the grave, then we won't be able to overcome our challenges.

With man it is impossible, but with God all things are possible. We serve a God who is, not only living, but He operates with no limitations, no boundaries or restrictions. We can look back at the Word of God and see that He has power, authority, and strength over everything and everyone. He created the heavens and earth. He parted the Red Sea. He spoke to nature and it had no choice but to obey. He commanded a den full of hungry lions not to touch Daniel, and they listened. The Lord commanded a huge fish to swallow Jonah, and to keep him in its belly for three days and three nights unharmed, and it listened. Pharaoh couldn't stand against Him. Goliath couldn't stand against the power of God. The prophets of Baal were no match for the Lord. The devil has been defeated and will always be defeated because our God is Almighty. Our God is all powerful and there is none who can stand against him. As children of God, we have every reason to rejoice and declare Romans 8:31 (NIV), "What, then, shall we say in response to these things? If God is for us, who can be against us?"

When we need divine strength from above, we can call on a God who has no limits. There is no limit to His strength. There is no limit to His wisdom and knowledge. There is no limit to His patience, love, and mercy.

Psalm 145:8-9 (NKJV), "[8] The Lord is gracious and full of compassion, slow to anger and great in mercy. [9] The Lord is good to all, and His tender mercies are over all His works."

God works beyond the limits of man, so be encouraged to call on the Lord for strength when the mountain in front of you looks daunting. Our God can move mountains, He can part seas, speak to nature, and shut the mouths of hungry lions.

PRAYER

Dear God

Your word tells me in Isaiah 40:29 (NKJV) that, "He give power to the weak, And to those who have no might He increases strength."

In my weakness, give me strength Lord Jesus. I thank you for the privilege of being able to approach Your throne of grace knowing that You love and care for me. Lord, when I am weighed down with the cares of life, be my strength. When I feel as though I am being crushed by my troubles, be my strength Lord. Strengthen me to stand strong when my faith is wavering. Strengthen me in my moments of weakness. I pray that the Holy Spirit would remind me, Father, that Your strength is made perfect when all of my strength is gone. You are all-powerful. I pray that you would equip me to handle all of life's difficulties. I am strong in You. I am strong with you Lord and I can only overcome because of You, King Jesus.

Holy Spirit, strengthen my faith. The Word of God tells me in Philippians 4:13 (NKJV) that, "I can do all things through Christ who strengthens me." Lord, I believe that through You, I can overcome and have victory in every area of my life. I believe that through You, I will have the strength to stand, even when confronted by lions like Daniel or by a fiery furnace like the three Hebrew boys. Lord, in their weakness and in their helpless state, You were in control and You delivered them in their hour of need. I trust you to do the same for me, even today.

Lord, I believe in your wonder-working power. I believe that the blood of Jesus Christ still has power today. The blood of Jesus Christ still has the power to deliver, to heal, to protect, and defend me and my family from the devil.

Father, strengthen me and help me to become a believer who is fearless and bold because of You. When voices of fear and doubt attempt to drown my faith, I pray that the Holy Spirit will remind me that Your grace is sufficient and Your strength is made perfect in my weakness.

Your Word in Psalm 46:1 (NIV) reminds me that, "God is our refuge and strength, an ever-present help in trouble." Thank you for always being there for me, Lord. I praise You for your consistency because time and time again You have provided me with all that I need to keep standing in faith. You are, and You have always been, faithful to deliver me from all of my cares and troubles.

You are worthy to be praised, Lord, because You have never been defeated. You have never lost a battle and the victory belongs to You, Jesus.

May Your name be lifted high always. I thank you for your goodness.

In Jesus' name I pray,

Amen.

GOD'S COVERING

As children of God, there are certain things that we need daily from the Lord. We need His mercy each and every day. We need His grace and favour each and every day, and we definitely need His protection. No matter how skilled you are, no matter how wealthy you are, you can never protect yourself from the attacks of the devil. That's why Psalm 34:19 (ESV) says, "Many are the afflictions of the righteous, but the Lord delivers him out of them all." Many will be the challenges you face over the course of your life. Many will be the obstacles that come up against you as you grow older. However, here is the key thing we need to remember: the Lord delivers us out of them all, not your ability, not your wealthy friends, not your ingenuity. It is the Lord God Almighty who can deliver you from every affliction.

It's only Jesus who can effectively block every arrow sent by the enemy. It's only Jesus who can disturb the devil's plans over your life. It's only Jesus who can expose the traps set before you. So, our attitude, as we wake up, go to sleep, leave our homes, and go about our business, must be one of thanksgiving and praise. We ought to rejoice that we are under the watchful eye of God Almighty. We ought to rejoice because, as God's children, we are covered by a heavenly host of angels.

The Bible says in Psalm 46:1 (NKJV), "God is our refuge and strength, a very present help in trouble." Our protection, our refuge, our strength is in the Lord. Don't wait until trouble comes knocking for you to realize that you need God. Don't wait until you're under attack from the devil before you realize, and acknowledge, that God is your best form of protection and defence.

There are many dangers in this world. You will never fail to find something that threatens your health, your peace of mind, or even your physical safety. This is why its so important that your prayer everyday should be that the Lord will continue to watch over you. May He protect us and keep us always! We should pray for strength and courage so that we may not be afraid or terrified by the afflictions of life. May the Lord go with us. May He go before us, and may He continually cover us.

PRAYER

Dear Lord,

I pray for supernatural protection over my life. I ask for divine protection for my family. Your Word tells me that You are a stronghold in the day of trouble. You are my refuge and my strength. You are the lion of the tribe of Judah. I plead the blood of Jesus Christ to form a hedge of protection around my home. I invite

Your presence into my life, into my home, and into my heart, King Jesus. I know that there is safety in Your presence and I pray that You will block every attack from the devil over my life. I pray that You would cancel every plan of the enemy Lord as I stand on your word and believe that, "no weapon formed against me shall prosper..." according to Isaiah 54:17 (NKJV).

I declare, through the authority that's in the mighty name of Jesus Christ, the living Son of God, that no weapon formed against my family or I will prosper. I declare through the authority that's in the mighty name of Jesus Christ, that no attack from the devil, no plan, no trap that is set, no plot or scheme will prosper because I am covered by the blood of Jesus. My family is covered. My home is covered. My life is covered. I am covered by the miracle-working blood of Jesus.

Lord, I stand and believe in Your Word that says in Psalm 91:7 (NKJV), "A thousand may fall at your side, and ten thousand at your right hand; but it shall not come near you." I believe this, Lord. I believe that no evil or darkness shall come near me because of You. You are the Most High God, the King of Kings, and the Lord of Lords.

I confess and I believe Your Word that says in Psalm 91:10-11 (NKJV), "¹⁰ No evil shall befall you, Nor shall any plague come near your dwelling; ¹¹ For He shall give His angels charge over you, To keep you in all your ways."

God, Your Word is true and everlasting. I stand in faith on Your Word. No evil will befall me or my family. No plague will come near my home or my body, in Jesus' name. Even though I may not see it with my natural eyes, I believe Your Word that tells me, You give Your angels charge over me and my family. You have charge over my life, Lord, and I praise you for being a God who is faithful to deliver those who trust in Him.

All my cares and worries, I give them to You. I surrender it all to You, because You are the One who neither sleeps nor slumbers. Lord Jesus, You are ever faithful. You are my hiding place. I ask for Your protection and covering over my life. I ask for Your covering over my family and loved ones. Although there is uncertainty in this world, there is fear and many unsettling things, I believe that You are a God who knows the beginning and the end. I believe that You are a God who provides shelter to Your children. You're the one who was, who is, and who will be, the God of Abraham, Isaac, and Jacob. Although I do not know what tomorrow or the future may hold, I do know that Your Word says in Psalm 37:25 (NKJV), "I have been young, and now am old; Yet I have not seen the righteous forsaken, nor his descendants begging bread."

Lord, Your Word in Jeremiah 17:7-8 (NKJV) says, "7 Blessed is the man who trusts in the Lord, and whose hope is the Lord. 8 For he shall be like a tree planted by the waters, which spreads out its roots by the river, and will not fear when heat comes; but its leaf will be green And will not be anxious in the year of drought, Nor will not cease from yielding fruit."

I declare that my trust is in the Lord. I declare that I am like a tree planted by the waters, and I am rooted in Jesus Christ. All the honour belongs to You. I am praying at this time because I need You. I need Your protection and I need Your covering. I look to You for direction. I look to You for counsel. Cover me, God. Thank You for hearing my prayer.

Amen.

GIVE THANKS

There are times when we ought to thank God, not only for what He has done but for who He is. Our God stands high and mighty above every idol and everything created. There is none who is greater than him or equal to him. God the Father is set apart, holy, and righteous. I wonder how many of us are truly in awe of the beauty of God? How many of us understand that he is worthy of our praise by virtue of Him being who He is?

The prophet Isaiah emphasized the incredible power and the omniscience of God Almighty in Isaiah 40:12-14 (ESV):

> *"12 Who has measured the waters in the hollow of his hand and marked off the heavens with a span enclosed the dust of the earth in a measure and weighed the mountains in scales and the hills in a balance? 13 Who has measured the Spirit of the Lord, or what man shows him his counsel? 14 Whom did he consult, and who made him understand? Who taught him the path of justice, and taught him knowledge, and showed him the way of understanding?"*

Isaiah 40:18 (ESV) goes on to say, "To whom then will you liken God, or what likeness compare with him?" We need to be aware that God really is almighty and all-powerful. He regulates all things, all creatures, and all of humanity. So great is Our Lord, that He measured the waters, the heavens, and even the dust of the earth. That is true greatness.

It should be noted that Isaiah 40:14 (ESV) asks the question, "Whom did he consult, and who made him understand? Who taught him the path of justice, and taught him knowledge, and showed him the way of understanding?" God doesn't need enlightening, for He is all-knowing. He doesn't need to be taught the right way, because He is the Creator. He is right. He is holy. He is righteous. He doesn't need the best scientists and the best minds of this world to make decisions. All power is in His hands.

May we acknowledge God for who He truly is – the Almighty One! We must adore Him for being so powerful yet so tender and caring to us. He is mighty to change and shift the entire universe, yet He is filled with compassion and love for us as His children. Will you open your heart and just take a moment to pray and thank Him for being who He is in your life?

PRAYER

Heavenly Father,

You are He who holds all of creation in His hands. I thank You for Your goodness. I thank You for loving me, sustaining me, and giving me life. You gave Your only begotten Son, Jesus Christ, so that I may live and not perish. So that I may not be destroyed, but rather, be saved. Thank You, Almighty God, for Your precious Son who died on a cross for me. I can now say that I am redeemed, I can say that I am forgiven and I am loved all because of you, King Jesus.

Lord, You deserve all glory for Your awesome power, there is none like you. No one else but you could measure the waters in each and every ocean, in each river, and in all of the seas of the earth. I praise You because there is no limit to Your abilities. There is nothing that You cannot do. Just as the Book of Isaiah asks, whom did You consult to enlighten You? Who was it that taught You knowledge? No one. There is no one who can enlighten You because You are an all-knowing God. No one can teach You anything because You are filled with infinite wisdom. Your ways are higher than mine. Your thoughts are higher than my thoughts. You are a God of great power, might, and strength. I adore You and praise Your name because if You never loved me, if You had never saved me, then, Father, where would I be?

Your Word says that You are enthroned above the circle of the earth. Angels surround Your glorious throne and sing, "Holy, holy, holy to the Lord God Almighty." There are no words to properly describe You Lord. You are infinite in wisdom and Your supernatural power is limitless.

Today I offer up my praises to You. There is nothing else that I can give You but my heart, my praise, and my adoration. You are my unfailing protector who gives me an eternal home. You are a God who watches over me and my family. I praise You, for You have never let me down. There is no one else like You, Father. I thank You, King Jesus, for being my rock and pillar. Thank You for being my rescue. I will rejoice always. I will give you thanks in all circumstances. You have a plan for my life that is divine and for a greater purpose, so I trust that all of my steps are ordered by You. I have confidence in Your Word that tells me to approach the throne of grace boldly. Father, I have confidence in Your Word that tells me if I ask anything according to Your will, You will hear me.

Thank You Lord. Thank You for being good to me. Thank You for being patient with me. Your Word says in Psalm 4:1 (NIV), "Answer me when I call to you, my righteous God. Give me relief from my distress; have mercy on me and hear my prayer." I trust and believe in You, King Jesus. I believe that You will answer me when I call out Your name. You offer me relief from distress. You offer wholeness from loneliness and insecurities. You offer me love and acceptance when the world would choose to condemn me. For that, I am thankful, and I rejoice. King Jesus, in Your Word

You say that You came so that I may have life and have it abundantly. I thank You for dying on the cross for me. You died to set me free from my sins. Thank You for Your sacrifice so that I may be with You in all of eternity. I pray that my relationship with You will continue to be strengthened day by day. Thank You for hearing this prayer.

In Jesus' name I pray,

Amen.

GOD WILL ORDER YOUR STEPS

Our steps are ordered by the Lord. This means nothing just happens. God has ordered your time in the lions' den, but He has also ordered your time to cross the Red Sea. God has ordered your time in the fiery furnace. However, He has also ordered your time to feast, as He prepares a table for you, in the presence of your enemies. The God of heaven is in control. It's not a matter of our timing. It's not a matter of our skill. It's not luck. It's all about God's plan, His will, and His perfect timing.

The Bible speaks of this in several scriptures:

Psalm 37:23-24 (NKJV) "²³ The steps of a good man are ordered by the Lord, and He delights in his way. ²⁴ Though he fall, he shall not be utterly cast down; for the Lord upholds him with His hand."

Proverbs 16:9 (NKJV) "A man's heart plans his way, but the Lord directs his steps."

Psalm 119:133 (NKJV) "Direct my steps by Your word, and let no iniquity have dominion over me."

Psalm 23:3 (NKJV) "He restores my soul; He leads me in the paths of righteousness for His name's sake."

Repeatedly in the Bible, we are told that the steps of a good man are ordered by the Lord. We're told that the Lord directs our steps. Sometimes it may be tough, because we don't always know what God's next step is for our lives. We may feel that not knowing means that the Lord isn't directing our steps. However, this is not the case. When we don't know what our next step is or where it should be, Psalm 119:105 (ESV) says, "Your word is a lamp to my feet and a light to my path," meaning that you can be directed through faith by reading the Word of God. So, do not be fearful if you don't know every step the Lord has for you. Rather, trust in Him. Trust in His Word.

PRAYER

My Lord,

I thank You for ordering my steps. Thank You for being my Good Shepherd. You are the one who leads me through the valley of the shadow of death. And You also lead me to lie down in green pastures and beside the still waters. I am grateful that I have You to lead me through the hard and painful seasons of life. I am grateful for Your hand that is over me and ensuring that I don't walk into destruction.

I surrender to You. I invite You to take full control. Guide me in my decisions. Guide me in my thinking.

Guide me in all that I may do. Whether I am at work or at home, I invite You, Lord Jesus, to be my guide. Whether I am with friends or with family, I ask that You guide all my interactions, because only under Your guidance can I have peace in my heart. I pray that the voice of the Holy Spirit will be strong and distinct in my life, so that I may discern Your voice from my own selfish desires.

Holy Spirit give me the strength and boldness to walk, to act, and to obey God's will for my life. I want to always say "yes" to You, Lord Jesus. I want to have a heart that is willing and yielded to You.

Remove all fear and confusion from my life. Remove everything that will hinder me from walking in Your way. I rebuke the spirit of fear, in the name of Jesus. I refuse to be fearful in any area of my life. Fill my mind with Your Word. Let there be a deep persuasion in my heart to spend more time in the Word of God, meditating on the Bible. Let my heart be so filled with the Word of God that there may be no room for any sin. Where I am unstable, steady my feet. Where I am indecisive, give me clarity and peace of mind. I pray that You will hold me steadfast. I pray that You place me on steady ground. Destroy every worry, every trace of fear, and all anxiety from my life.

I desire to live in the truth of Your Word that says in Joshua 1:9 (NIV), "Have I not commanded you? Be strong and courageous. Do not be afraid; do not be discouraged, for the Lord your God will be with you wherever you go." I pray that I will not be afraid or discouraged. You, Lord, will be with me wherever I go, ordering my steps and leading me. I will obey Your Word and walk by faith, because the God of all power is leading my path. Give me the grace to always trust in Your direction each and every day. Lead me, Lord Jesus. If God is for me, then who can be against me? Who can stand before my Almighty Lord and Saviour, Jesus Christ?

Lead me, Father, because on my own, I will not always make the right decisions. I will not always make good decisions. But if You are directing my steps, I know that Your amazing grace and favour will surround me. I need Your wisdom, Lord. I submit to Your will, and I submit to all Your ways. I will trust in the Lord with all my heart. I will not lean on my own understanding. I will acknowledge You, Father, in all my ways, because when I do, You will make straight my paths. I praise You, the God of the universe, the Creator of the heavens and the earth. I will forever sing Your praises and adore Your holy name. Thank You for hearing this prayer.

In the mighty name of Jesus Christ I pray,

Amen.

PEACE BEYOND UNDERSTANDING

There are several promises of peace that are found in the Bible. Peace is a gift freely given to us through Jesus Christ. The prophet Isaiah declared that Jesus Christ would be the Prince of Peace. Therefore, there is no peace in the absence of Christ. There is no peace unless there is Jesus Christ.

Isaiah 54:10 (NKJV) says, " 'For the mountains shall depart and the hills be removed, but My kindness shall not depart from you, nor shall My covenant of peace be removed,' says the Lord, who has mercy on you." This is a great promise that tells us that, although the mountains and hills may be removed, God's kindness will not be removed, nor will His promise of peace. In other words, even if the most unlikely of situations were to happen, God's promise of kindness and peace will not be removed. We should take comfort in this. The knowledge that your world can suddenly be turned upside down but that changes nothing when it comes to God's promise of kindness and peace.

It's only when Jesus Christ is at the centre of your heart that you can experience true peace. It's only in the presence of Jesus Christ that you can say to your soul, "It is well. Peace, be still." Only the presence of Our Lord, Jesus Christ, can provide your soul with a deep calmness. Only His holy presence can provide us with a quiet confidence, a confidence that declares, "It is well." Whatever you are in need of today, remember to search for, pray for, and ask for the holy peace of God to be over your mind, body, and soul.

PRAYER

King Jesus,

You are great and mighty and worthy to be praised. I adore Your holy name, and I ask that Your presence will surround me. I pray that a divine, heavenly peace might fall upon me. May a Godly peace wrap me up and cover me. Keep me covered from the fear that's in this world. Keep me safe, Lord, and protect me. Protect me from anything that threatens to trouble my mind. Protect me from anything that threatens to trouble my heart. Lord, defend me from anything that threatens to discourage me. Father, I pray that you will help me so that nothing in this world will affect me and cause me to lose my peace.

I stand on Your promises of peace today. Your Word says in Psalm 29:11 (NKJV), "The Lord will give strength to His people; the Lord will bless His people with peace." Lord I receive this blessing of peace.

Give me the grace to overcome the troubles I face. May Your hand be over my life and lift me up whenever

I feel overwhelmed. I place my confidence in You, my Lord, You are my rescue and my deliverer. You will uplift me and protect me from all harm. Lord, today I call You Wonderful Counsellor, Mighty God, Everlasting Father, Prince of Peace. I believe in Your word that says in John 16:33 (NIV), "I have told you these things, so that in me you may have peace. In this world you will have trouble. But take heart! I have overcome the world."

As Your child, washed and saved by Your powerful blood, I will take heart. Even if I face trouble and disappointments, I have overcome because of You, Lord. Heavenly Father, I pray that Your peace may be like a shield around me. May it protect me from being discouraged and from losing hope. May Your peace put aside all anxious thoughts. I pray, Lord Jesus, that You will help me to take life one day at a time and to trust You always.

Give me the grace to accept the things that I cannot change and to be at peace. I pray for peace beyond human understanding when it comes to anything outside of my control. May I be at peace because, ultimately, You are the one who controls all things. Give me the wisdom, Lord, to live a life that is peaceful with all people. Let me be someone who is not angry or contentious with others but I pray that You would give me a peaceful and kind character.

Lord, I pray for a spirit that is always thankful for the gift of life, a spirit that enjoys the time that You have afforded me here on earth with my loved ones.

You, Lord Jesus, are the same yesterday, today, and forever. You are the same everlasting Father who said that You will fight for me and I will hold my peace. So great is Your love that You have numbered the hairs on my head. You knew me before I was formed in my mother's womb and You still care for me today. Lord Jesus, I am eternally grateful for your unending love and mercy.

Father, I desire to be alone with You and dwell in Your presence daily. I desire close communion with You. It's only in You that I can be revived and refreshed in my soul. It's only in Your presence that I can experience a peace that is beyond all comprehension. Only You, Lord Jesus, are able to clear away all feelings of stress and anxiety. Your word says in Matthew 11:28 (NKJV), "Come to Me, all you who labour and are heavy laden, and I will give you rest." I come to You today, Master. Give me rest and remove all my burdens.

Thank You for hearing my prayer.

In the precious name of Jesus Christ I pray,

Amen.

PRAYER FOR PROTECTION (PSALM 91)

When it comes to the assurance of God's protection, Psalm 91 is a chapter that offers us great hope and direction. It gives us assurance when it comes to where we should look and go to regarding safety.

¹He who dwells in the secret place of the Most High
Shall abide under the shadow of the Almighty.
²I will say of the Lord, 'He is my refuge and my fortress;
My God, in Him I will trust.'
³Surely He shall deliver you from the snare of the fowler
And from the perilous pestilence.
⁴He shall cover you with His feathers,
And under His wings you shall take refuge;
His truth shall be your shield and buckler.
⁵You shall not be afraid of the terror by night,
Nor of the arrow that flies by day,
⁶Nor of the pestilence that walks in darkness,
Nor of the destruction that lays waste at noonday.
⁷A thousand may fall at your side,
And ten thousand at your right hand;
But it shall not come near you.
⁸Only with your eyes shall you look,
And see the reward of the wicked.
⁹Because you have made the Lord, who is my refuge,

Even the Most High, your dwelling place,
¹⁰No evil shall befall you,
Nor shall any plague come near your dwelling;
¹¹For He shall give His angels charge over you,
To keep you in all your ways.
¹²In their hands they shall bear you up,
Lest you dash your foot against a stone.
¹³You shall tread upon the lion and the cobra,
The young lion and the serpent you
Shall trample underfoot.
¹⁴'Because he has set his love upon Me,
Therefore I will deliver him;
I will set him on high, because he has Known My name.
¹⁵He shall call upon Me, and I will answer him;
I will be with him in trouble;
I will deliver him and honour him.
¹⁶With long life I will satisfy him,
And show him My salvation.'
(Psalm 91:1-16 NKJV)

PRAYER

My dearest Heavenly Father,

You are the Most High. You are the Almighty One. Father, I pray that I will always abide under Your shadow. I thank You for always being near to me and I pray that I will continually draw closer to You. I confess that You are my safe place, and You are my strong tower. You are my God. I trust You to be with me always and to be my defender. You, Lord Jesus, are faithful. I trust and believe that You will strengthen me and protect me from the evil one.

Just as David said to the Lord in Psalm 27:4-5 (NKJV), "⁴ One *thing* I have desired of the Lord, that will I seek: That I may dwell in the house of the Lord all the days of my life, to behold the beauty of the Lord, and to inquire in His temple. ⁵ For in the time of trouble He shall hide me in His pavilion; In the secret place of His tabernacle He shall hide me; He shall set me high upon a rock."

Father, I desire to live a life that is close to You. When I am close to You, Your Word promises me safety and protection. I declare today, Lord Jesus, You are my shelter. You are my safety net. You are the only one I trust and I thank You for hearing my prayer. In the mighty name of Jesus Christ I pray,

Amen.

THE JOY OF THE LORD WILL STRENGTHEN YOU

Psalm 118:24 (NKJV)
"This is the day the Lord has made;
we will rejoice and be glad in it."

What else can we do but rejoice and be glad in the day that the Lord has made? What else can we do but rejoice that the Lord has given us a new day, a fresh opportunity to live for Him? We have so many reasons to be joyful. Rejoice in this day that the Lord has made because, as a child of God, you have a deliverer, you have a way maker, and you have the power to overcome whatever you face because you have Jesus Christ. Through Jesus Christ, you have the strength to endure anything, the faith to withstand any storm and the firepower required to defeat the devil.

Psalm 118:24 (NKJV), "This is the day the Lord has made; we will rejoice and be glad in it." This verse is not a suggestion but rather a statement, a declaration. Don't simply rejoice when things are well or when everything is good, but rejoice each day, no matter what meets you at sunrise. Remember what God's word says in Jeremiah 29:11 (NKJV), "For I know the thoughts that I think toward you, says the Lord, thoughts of peace and not of evil, to give you a future and a hope." Rejoice and be glad, because God has plans for you, plans to prosper you, plans for good things. This is what we should be glad and rejoice in. We have a God who cares, a God who wants the best for us. Rejoice and be glad that the Lord God Almighty wants good things for you. Your present circumstances may not be perfect, but you should always be able to find just one reason to rejoice and be glad in this day that the Lord has made.

PRAYER

Heavenly Father,

You are a great and mighty God. You are my Redeemer, Lord Jesus, the One who has delivered me from sin and led me to freedom. Your Word says in Psalm 118:24 (NKJV), "This is the day the Lord has made; we will rejoice and be glad in it." I will indeed rejoice and be glad in this day that You have made Lord. Thank You for this new day. Thank You for the air I am breathing. Thank You for simply giving me the ability to praise You.

Forgive me for the times that I have not rejoiced about the grace and goodness You show me. Forgive me for taking You for granted. Holy Spirit, I am asking that You would help me when I feel tired and overwhelmed. Help me and give me joy and strength during those difficult moments where I don't see an end to my troubles. Help me, Holy Spirit, so that I may always find a reason to rejoice. Open my eyes so that I can see all of the many blessings that the Lord has given to me.

Lord, help me so that I may not let the world steal my joy. Help me to remember that I have victory in Jesus. I refuse to let the devil steal, kill, and destroy my joy. I am holding on to the promise that Jesus Christ came to this earth so that I might have life more abundantly.

I rejoice today because of the sovereignty of my Father, my Heavenly Father, who is in absolute control of everything. There is nothing that takes place in my life that You, my God, have not allowed to happen. I find strength knowing that the Sovereign God of all creation works all things together for my good. I rejoice because You, Lord Jesus, have stripped away my old garments of sin. You have clothed me in Your love and tender mercies. I thank You, King Jesus, because no matter how difficult or painful things may get, You will always be with me.

I bless Your name for You have given me the promise that even if I walk through the valley of the shadow of death, I will fear no evil, for You are with me. Your rod and staff, they comfort me. Thank You for Your presence that surrounds me. Your holy presence protects me and keeps me safe. John 14:2 (NKJV) says, "In my Father's house are many mansions; if it were not so, I would have told you. I go to prepare a place for you." I thank You, Lord Jesus, for this promise, a promise that I can rejoice and be glad in. I rejoice in knowing that You have prepared a place for me in eternity.

Psalm 119:162 (NKJV) says, "I rejoice at Your word as one who finds great treasure." Father, thank You for Your precious Word that provides me with comfort and assurance. Your Word provides me with so many reasons to be joyful and glad. Your Word tells me not to fear, for You are with me. Your Word tells me that if I trust in You, You will keep me in perfect peace. Your Word tells me that You order my steps and You go before me. I can find many reasons to rejoice when I read Your Word, O God. May Your Word always live inside my heart. May I always meditate on Your Word, Lord.

Father, Mark 11:24 (ESV) says, "Therefore I tell you, whatever you ask in prayer, believe that you have received it, and it will be yours." I thank You for the promise that the God of heaven listens my prayers. I am grateful that You are a caring God. You have infinite wisdom and power, yet You still take the time to hear my prayers. For this reason, I will rejoice. I thank You, Lord, for every single thing You do. Holy Spirit, help me to always live in a manner that gives God all of the glory and praise, a manner that is joyful and thankful. Thank You for hearing this prayer, Father. Praise be unto You.

Amen.

HELP IN THE MIDST OF DISTRESS

Jonah prayed from a place of darkness and deep distress. He prayed from a place where he had no other choice but to turn to God. He prayed from a place where he had nowhere else to go, nowhere else to turn but to the Lord. He was completely powerless. In this life, we can also easily find ourselves in a similar position. Whether it's because of disobedience or no fault of our own, each one of us will at one point find ourselves "in the belly of a fish." When Jonah found himself in this position, he did the only thing he could do, and that is to turn to the Lord in prayer. Jonah 2:1-10 (ESV), the bible reads:

> [1] *Then Jonah prayed to the Lord his God from the belly of the fish,* [2] *saying, "I called out to the Lord, out of my distress, and he answered me; out of the belly of Sheol I cried, and you heard my voice.*
> [3] *For you cast me into the deep, into the heart of the seas, and the flood surrounded me;*
> *all your waves and your billows passed over me.*
> [4] *Then I said, 'I am driven away from your sight; yet I shall again look upon your holy temple.'*
> [5] *The waters closed in over me to take my life; the deep surrounded me; weeds were wrapped about my head*
> [6] *at the roots of the mountains. I went down to the land*

*whose bars closed upon me forever; yet you brought up
my life from the pit, O Lord my God.*
*⁷ When my life was fainting away, I remembered the
Lord, and my prayer came to you, into your holy temple.*
*⁸ Those who pay regard to vain idols forsake their hope of
steadfast love.*
*⁹ But I with the voice of thanksgiving will sacrifice to
you; what I have vowed I will pay. Salvation belongs to
the Lord!"*
*¹⁰ And the Lord spoke to the fish, and it vomited Jonah
out upon the dry land.*

Now you may be able to relate to some of the feelings
of deep distress that Jonah experienced. You may be
feeling completely powerless and as though there is no
way out of your situation. If that is the case, then you
should be encouraged by the Word of God. In Jonah
2:2 (ESV), Jonah said, "I called out to the Lord, out of
my distress, and he answered me…" God can do the
same for us today. He will do the same for us today.
In our moments of distress, in our moments of pain,
we can call on the Lord. It doesn't matter what the
situation you are facing is today, call out to the Lord!
Regardless of how bad things appear to be, call out to
Jesus Christ and He will answer you. You will find Him
to be a saviour and a marvellous help.

PRAYER

My dear Father,

You are a holy God, worthy to be praised and honoured.

I pray, Lord, that in every situation I face, may I always have confidence in the knowledge that You are in control. May I always have the faith to know that if I call out to You when I need help, You will answer me. You are God above all, above every principality, above every ruler, and even above my situation. You sit high on the throne, Lord, with all power. It's You that I turn to. It's Your name that I call. It's Your Word that I hold on to.

I pray that every test and every trial that I go through in this life may bring me closer to You. May it result in good things happening within me. When I go through painful situations, I pray that I will remember that You are a wonderful comforter and the ultimate healer. If I go through tough times, I pray that I will become stronger in faith and bold in my life as a believer. Father, I pray that You will produce in me a character that is pleasing to You. Produce in me stronger faith, a prayerful spirit, a deeper desire to know You and to walk with You.

When I am in trouble, I pray that the Holy Spirit will help me turn to the cross. Help me to always turn to Jesus Christ first. Let my first instinct, my first reaction, be to call on the name of Jesus Christ. I pray that You will see me in my struggle, Lord. May Your loving-kindness and compassion meet me at my point of need. I pray that Your glorious strength will meet me at the point of my weakness. Your Word, in Psalm 121:1-2 (NIV) says, "[1] I lift up my eyes to the mountains — where does my help come from? [2] My help comes from the Lord, the Maker of heaven and earth."

My help does indeed come from You, Lord, the Creator of the heavens and earth. So, when the days feel too hard, when I am low in my spirit, I will lift up my eyes to You, King Jesus. I will call out to You for help. I will continue to trust that in the midst of it all, You will never leave me nor forsake me. You, as the Good Shepherd, will never leave me to fend for myself.

I will forever hold on to Psalm 121:7-8 (NKJV), which says, "[7] The Lord shall preserve you from all evil; He shall preserve your soul. [8] The Lord shall preserve your going out and your coming in from this time forth, and even forevermore."

I believe You are more than able to rescue me and save me. You are God over every situation. You are God over all things and there is none who stands above you. You are a wonder-working God who can move mountains, split the seas and do the impossible.

I pray that the Holy Ghost will stand with me always. I bless Your name. Thank You for hearing my prayer.

In the mighty name of Jesus I pray,

Amen.

A HEART OF WORSHIP

Have you ever heard a song that just speaks to you, and I mean it speaks to the very core of your heart? Music is powerful, because it can create or change an atmosphere. And when I'm talking about music, I'm talking about worshiping God.

Psalm 105:2 (NKJV) says, "Sing to Him, sing psalms to Him; Talk of all His wondrous works!"

Is this something that you do often? Do you sing of God's wonderful works? Do you praise the Lord for his goodness? Do you worship God because He is holy and deserves to be praised?

The Bible says, "Talk of all His wondrous works!"

For me personally, there is one particular song that resonates with me. It's a song called "Made a Way", and it was performed by a man called Travis Greene. It resonates with me because, if I look back at some of the things I've overcome, it's only God that could have made a way for me.

A few lines from the song read as follows:

Standing here not knowing how we'll get through this test
But holding onto faith You know that
Nothing can catch You by surprise
You've got this figured out and You're watching us now
But when it looks as if we can't win
You wrap us in Your arms and step in
And everything we need You supply
You got this in control
And now we know that

You made a way
When our backs were against the wall
And it looked as if it was over
You made a way
And we're standing here
Only because You made a way
You made a way

I don't know about you, but there have been times where it looked as though I wouldn't overcome what was in front of me. There have been times where the mountain was high and the sea that was before me was daunting. But God is faithful. God made a way for me. God provided for me, and God helped me.

I want to encourage you to do as Psalm 105:2 (NKJV) says, "Sing to Him, sing psalms to Him; Talk of all His wondrous works!"

If God has done something for you – and for each of us, the Lord has certainly done something for us, we ought to worship him! We ought to talk about His wondrous works.

The book of Revelation gives us a glimpse into heaven, and I want you to notice how worshipping God is a constant activity in heaven.

Revelation 4:8-11 (NKJV):

> [8] The four living creatures, each having six wings, were full of eyes around and within. And they do not rest day or night, saying:
>
> *"Holy, holy, holy,*
> *Lord God Almighty,*
> *Who was and is and is to come!"*
>
> [9] Whenever the living creatures give glory and honour and thanks to Him who sits on the throne, who lives forever and ever, [10] the twenty-four elders fall down before Him who sits on the throne and worship Him who lives forever and ever, and cast their crowns before the throne, saying:
>
> [11] *"You are worthy, O Lord,*
> *To receive glory and honour and power;*
> *For You created all things,*
> *And by Your will they exist and were created."*

Let us worship the Lord because He is Holy, because He is good and righteous. Let us worship Him, because He is worthy of our adoration.

PRAYER

My Lord, my God,

Your Word in Psalm 105:3-5 (NKJV) says:

> ³ *"Glory in His holy name;*
> *Let the hearts of those rejoice who seek the Lord!*
>
> ⁴ *Seek the Lord and His strength;*
> *Seek His face evermore!*
>
> ⁵ *Remember His marvellous works which He has done,*
> *His wonders, and the judgments of His mouth"*

Father, I praise You today. I praise You because You are a God who is merciful and gracious, slow to anger and abounding in steadfast love and faithfulness.

I praise You, God, because You are the God of light and in You there is no darkness at all. You are holy and righteous. You are an awesome God. I praise You, Lord, because You are not a man, that You should lie. Your ways are higher than our ways, and Your thoughts are higher than our thoughts.

Lord, I pray that the Holy Spirit will help me and quicken my spirit so that I can worship the Lord in spirit and in truth. Give me a heart of worship, a heart that seeks to praise and worship my Lord and Saviour, Jesus Christ, daily.

As I worship You, Lord, I am declaring that my life is in Your hands. As I worship You, King Jesus, I am rejoicing about the fact that You have saved me, You have redeemed me and set me free from bondage. As I worship You, Lord Jesus, I am declaring that it is well with me. It is well in my life because my King has risen from the grave. As I worship You, my Lord, I acknowledge that You are my strength, You are my hope and light.

Your Word in 1 Chronicles 16:23-27 (NKJV) says:

> 23 *"Sing to the Lord, all the earth;*
> *Proclaim the good news of His salvation from day to day.*
>
> 24 *Declare His glory among the nations,*
> *His wonders among all peoples.*
>
> 25 *For the Lord is great and greatly to be praised;*
> *He is also to be feared above all gods.*
>
> 26 *For all the gods of the peoples are idols,*
> *But the Lord made the heavens.*
>
> 27 *Honour and majesty are before Him;*
> *Strength and gladness are in His place."*

Father, I pray that worship may be a way of life for me. Let it be a daily practice for me, as I seek Your presence. Let my heart be a place that continually worships You. May my lips always sing Your praises. Let my home be a place of worship; a place where Your presence resides.

Lord, I praise You for Your protection. I praise You for Your provision. I thank You for always making a way for me whenever I have been backed into a corner. I thank You for always stepping in whenever I've needed You. Lord, I pray that I will be the kind of believer who will live according to Colossians 3:16 (NKJV) which says, "Let the word of Christ dwell in you richly in all wisdom, teaching and admonishing one another in psalms and hymns and spiritual songs, singing with grace in your hearts to the Lord."

Be glorified my King. You are worthy to be praised and worthy to be honoured. May Your name be lifted high forever and ever, King Jesus.

Thank you for hearing my prayer,

Amen.

GOD WILL GUARD YOU

Ephesians 6:13 (NKJV)
"Therefore take up the whole armour of God,
that you may be able to withstand in the evil day,
and having done all, to stand."

I would like to take a moment to deconstruct this verse and what it means to us as children of God.

The Bible says, "Therefore take up the whole armour of God." The first thing to notice is that this is an instruction. We are told to "take up" the whole armour of God. It's not a question of whether you can or cannot take this up... no, it's a clear instruction. This is something you need to do.

The second thing is that, you only need armour if you are in a war. You only need armour in battle. You only need armour when there is an opposing force coming against you.

When the Bible says "the whole armour," this says to me that there are multiple parts that need to be taken up. Anything other than the whole armour would leave you vulnerable, so it's important we follow this instruction and not only take up parts of the armour but the whole armour of God!

Now the second part half of Ephesians 6:13 (NKJV) says, "...that you may be able to withstand in the evil day, and having done all, to stand."

This statement has a level of certainty to it. You need to take up the whole armour of God so that you can withstand in the evil day. Now, in this part of the verse, I get the impression that the Bible is warning us. The Bible is warning us that there will be an evil day. A day when we will have to fight the forces of evil. However, if we are wearing the whole armour of God then we will be able to withstand anything the devil aims in our direction.

Now that we have a better understanding of this verse, I want to encourage you. Yes, you are in a war! If you are a true disciple of Christ, you will be at war. You're at war against the rulers, against the authorities, against the powers of this dark world and against the spiritual forces of evil in the heavenly realms.

However, the Word is central to your defensive stance, as well as your offensive stance, as a Christian.

So when you face the evil day, remember 2 Thessalonians 3:3 (NKJV), "But the Lord is faithful, who will establish you and guard you from the evil one."

When you face the evil day, remember Deuteronomy 31:6 (NKJV) says, "Be strong and of good courage, do not fear nor be afraid of them; for the Lord your God, He is the One who goes with you. He will not leave you nor forsake you."

When you face the evil day, remember Psalm 46:1 (NKJV) says, "God is our refuge and strength, A very present help in trouble."

So be encouraged, child of God. Do not fear when evil comes against you. The Lord is with you, and the promises of God should give you the confidence to be bold in the face of evil.

PRAYER

Lord Jesus,

You are my great defender. You are my mighty protector. Revelation 12:11 (NKJV) says, "And they overcame him by the blood of the Lamb and by the word of their testimony, and they did not love their lives to the death."

I am blessed because I am covered by Your blood, the precious blood of the Lamb of God.

Your Word tells me that I can overcome the devil by the blood of the Lamb and the word of my testimony. And so I plead for the blood of Jesus Christ over my life. I plead for the blood of Jesus Christ over my family.

The word of my testimony is that Jesus Christ is the King of Kings and the Lord of Lords. The word of my testimony is that Jesus Christ is victorious. Jesus Christ is triumphant, and greater is He who is in me than he who is in the world!

Lord Jesus, You have never lost a battle. There is none who can challenge You. So I firmly place my confidence in You. You are the reason why I am more than a conqueror. You are the reason why my heart is filled with boldness and courage.

Psalm 138:7-8 (NKJV) says: "[7] Though I walk in the midst of trouble, You will revive me; You will stretch out Your hand against the wrath of my enemies, and Your right hand will save me. [8] The Lord will perfect that which concerns me; Your mercy, O Lord, endures forever; Do not forsake the works of Your hands."

I am an encouraged by Your Word which tells me that You, my Lord, will perfect that which concerns me; You will straighten out everything crooked in my path. You will remove all obstacles, and You will certainly prepare a table before me in the presence of my enemies.

Be praised, Lord. You are an awesome God. I pray that you will stand with me always.

The Bible says in Isaiah 59:19 (NKJV): "So shall they fear the name of the Lord from the west, and His glory from the rising of the sun; When the enemy comes in like a flood, the Spirit of the Lord will lift up a standard against him."

I praise you, Lord Jesus, because when the enemy comes at me and my family You are faithful to block all of his attacks. The enemy cannot overwhelm me, because I am holding on to the promises in God's Word; promises that tell me that I have authority in Jesus' name. Promises that tell me that a thousand may fall at my side, ten thousand at my right hand, but it will not come near me.

Lord Jesus, I am at peace. I declare that there is no fear within me, because you have not given me a spirit of fear. You have given me a spirit of power, love, and a sound mind.

I can say that it is well with me, because you are for me Lord, and if God is for me, who can be against me? Who can stand against you, the Lion of the tribe of Judah? So great is your power and might that the earth is your footstool.

Thank you for faithfulness, my great deliverer. Thank you for hearing my prayer.

In Jesus' name I pray,

Amen.

NO TIME TO WASTE

Do you know what I've found? I have found that life is full of surprises. In fact, my walk with God has been full of surprises. I made plans, I wrote down my goals and dreams. I expected everything to go right; I expected things to go my way. However, our expectations and reality can often be very different. And the thing is, we can make plans, we can write down our goals and our targets, however, here's what the Bible says, Proverbs 19:21 (ESV), "Many are the plans in the mind of a man, but it is the purpose of the Lord that will stand."

Now there is a danger in making plans without acknowledging the fact that God is ultimately in control and that tomorrow is not promised. After all, the Bible does say in James 4:13-15 (ESV): [13] Come now, you who say, "Today or tomorrow we will go into such and such a town and spend a year there and trade and make a profit"— [14] yet you do not know what tomorrow will bring. What is your life? For you are a mist that appears for a little time and then vanishes. [15] Instead you ought to say, "If the Lord wills, we will live and do this or that."

Now how many of us really live like this, whereby we make our plans, yes, but still acknowledge that God has the final say? When was the last time you said, "If the Lord wills, I will live and do this or that"?

There is a parable in the Bible of a man who made many, many plans but paid no mind to God. His focus was only on the things he desired... his focus was only on the material things that he accumulated when instead his focus really should have been on Jesus Christ.

Luke 12:13-21 (NKJV):

> *13 Then one from the crowd said to Him, "Teacher, tell my brother to divide the inheritance with me." 14 But He said to him, "Man, who made Me a judge or an arbitrator over you?" 15 And He said to them, "Take heed and beware of covetousness, for one's life does not consist in the abundance of the things he possesses." 16 Then He spoke a parable to them, saying: "The ground of a certain rich man yielded plentifully. 17 And he thought within himself, saying, 'What shall I do, since I have no room to store my crops?' 18 So he said, 'I will do this: I will pull down my barns and build greater, and there I will store all my crops and my goods. 19 And I will say to my soul, "Soul, you have many goods laid up for many years; take your ease; eat, drink, and be merry." ' 20 But God said to him, 'Fool! This night your soul will be required of you; then whose will those things be which you have provided?' 21 "So is he who lays up treasure for himself, and is not rich toward God."*

People of God, learn this lesson. We only have so much time in this world, and we have no time to waste it!

Now don't get me wrong, it's good to be wise and save. It's good to make retirement plans and, it's good to work hard with your hands and build a better life for and your family. Those things are good. But it's crucial for you to invest in your relationship with God. It's crucial for you to invest in the treasures that are in heaven. It's crucial for you to live life knowing that eternity lasts forever, but this world is only passing by.

PRAYER

Dear Lord,

Have mercy on me. Forgive me if I have put more effort into the things of this world as opposed to heavenly things. Forgive me if I have invested more time in building things here on earth as opposed to storing up treasures in heaven.

Your Word in Matthew 6:19-21 (NKJV) says,

> *"[19] Do not lay up for yourselves treasures on earth, where moth and rust destroy and where thieves break in and steal, [20] but lay up for yourselves treasures in heaven, where neither moth nor rust destroys and where thieves do not break in and steal. [21] For where your treasure is, there your heart will be also."*

Lord, I pray that You will give me a heart that seeks heavenly treasures above earthly things. I pray that the material things of this world will not have any kind of hold on me. I pray that my eyes and heart will never be drawn to chase the riches or the silver and gold of this world.

Instead, King Jesus, I pray that I will be richly filled with the Holy Spirit. I pray that I will be richly filled with the love of God in my heart; a love that seeks to minister to the unsaved and help the poor. May I be richly filled with a love from God so that I can serve the body of Christ and do all I can to spread the good news of the gospel of Jesus Christ.

Father, help me to realize that earthly treasure, earthly crowns, are temporary, they are short-lived, and any riches in this world are perishable. However, I know that You, Lord Jesus, offer a greater treasure than anything on this earth.

Father, Your Word in James 1:12 (NKJV) says, "Blessed is the man who endures temptation; for when he has been approved, he will receive the crown of life which the Lord has promised to those who love Him."

Help me to endure the temptations of this world. Strengthen me, Holy Spirit, so that I can resist the advances of the devil because, in doing so, there is the reward of the crown of life.

Father, I desire to be rewarded with the crown of righteousness. Your Word, in 2 Timothy 4:8 (NKJV), says, "Finally, there is laid up for me the crown of righteousness, which the Lord, the righteous Judge, will give to me on that Day, and not to me only but also to all who have loved His appearing."

I pray that the Holy Spirit will help me and strengthen me to live a life that is pleasing to You, Lord Jesus. You are the only one who can offer eternal riches, eternal crowns, and blessings in Your presence forevermore.

And so, Father, I have decided to let go of this world. I choose to leave the luxuries afforded to me in this world so that I can focus on You, King Jesus. Let me not be distracted by the things of this world, or even by my own personal plans, but may I be forever engaged in the pursuit of righteousness.

You, Lord Jesus, are worth far more than all of the silver and gold on offer in this world. My true riches lie in You, and I rejoice because of that.

I honour You, and I lift your name on high.

Be glorified, Lord Jesus,

Amen.

A PASSION FOR PRAYER

If we desire to see God working in our lives, we need to pray. If we desire to see a transformation in our lives then prayer is essential.

If we desire to experience breakthrough victories in this life, then we need to pray. If we desire to experience the presence of God, if we want to develop and strengthen our relationship with God, then we need to talk to Him.

And how do you talk to Him? You pray! How often can you talk to Him? As often as you pray! How much time can you spend talking to Him? As much time as you spend in prayer.

James 5:13-18 (NKJV) is a powerful passage of scripture regarding prayer. The Bible reads:

13 Is anyone among you suffering? Let him pray. Is anyone cheerful? Let him sing psalms. 14 Is anyone among you sick? Let him call for the elders of the church, and let them pray over him, anointing him with oil in the name of the Lord. 15 And the prayer of faith will save the sick, and the Lord will raise him up. And if he has committed sins, he will be forgiven. ¹⁶ Confess your trespasses to one another, and pray for one another, that you may be healed. The effective, fervent prayer of a righteous man avails much. ¹⁷ Elijah was a man with a nature like ours, and he prayed earnestly that it would not rain; and it did not rain on the land for three years and six months. ¹⁸ And he prayed again, and the heaven gave rain, and the earth produced its fruit.

Look at how often the word pray is mentioned... But, more importantly, look at the reasons why we should pray.

Verse 13 asks, "Is anyone among you suffering? Let him pray." Verse 14 calls for the church elders to pray, if anyone is sick. Verse 15 goes on to say, "And the prayer of faith will save the sick," while verse 16 recommends us to "...pray for one another, that you may be healed. The effective, fervent prayer of a righteous man avails much."

Now let's focus on the last couple of verses in this passage of scripture, verse 17 and 18. Notice how the Bible says, "Elijah was a man with a nature like ours..."

The Amplified Bible translation for James 5:17 offers a detailed breakdown of what this nature is, as it reads, "Elijah was a man with a nature like ours [with the same physical, mental, and spiritual limitations and shortcomings], and he prayed intensely for it not to rain, and it did not rain on the earth for three years and six months."

Now why does the Bible mention this? Why is it important for us to know that Elijah was a man with a nature like ours?

I believe the reason for this is because many people may view Elijah as a rather unique or very special person, but the Bible is making it clear that Elijah was just like everyone else. He was just like anyone else.

Notice, in verse 17 and 18, that every time Elijah prayed something happened. Elijah, a man with a nature like ours, would pray for the rain to stop and it would. He would then pray for the heavens to open with rain, and it would rain.

Now I don't want to focus on Elijah, but I want to focus on his relationship with God. He prayed and God acted. He prayed and God answered.

My message to you is that you should focus on your relationship with God and pray. God still answers prayers. It may not be exactly how you want Him to answer, it may not be when you want Him to answer, but remember, "The effective, fervent prayer of the righteous man avails much."

PRAYER

Holy Spirit, help me to pray. Let prayer be my lifestyle. May prayer become a habitual practice for me. Holy Spirit, give me a heart that is devoted to prayer. Give me an insatiable desire for prayer and a hunger for daily communion with the Lord.

Holy Spirit, develop an appetite within me for Jesus Christ. Develop a hunger within me for Jesus, who is the bread of life. Let me thirst for Him, the One who offers living waters. Let there be a burning desire within me to fall on my knees and pray always.

Holy Spirit, strengthen me to pray without ceasing. Strengthen me to continue earnestly in prayer.

Philippians 4:6-7 (NKJV) says, "[6] Be anxious for nothing, but in everything by prayer and supplication, with thanksgiving, let your requests be made known to God; [7] and the peace of God, which surpasses all understanding, will guard your hearts and minds through Christ Jesus."

When I am anxious, worried or stressed, Holy Spirit, teach me to pray and cast my burdens on Jesus. When my mind is weighed down by the cares of life, Holy Spirit, help me to make my requests known to God and to trust Him. Ephesians 6:18 (NKJV) says, "Praying always with all prayer and supplication in the Spirit, being watchful to this end with all perseverance and supplication for all the saints."

Holy Ghost, quicken my spirit so that I may be able to pray in all occasions. Help me to rejoice always, to pray without ceasing and to give thanks in all circumstances. Open my eyes, Holy Spirit, so that I can see the beauty of prayer and communicating with God.

Father, as I pray and seek You, may You change my character, give me a patient heart, a thankful heart, and a heart filled with joy and peace. Lord, as I pray, as I state my requests to You, give me a heart that understands that You are a sovereign God who answers when the time is right. You are a God who has perfect timing. I will wait on You, King Jesus. I will wait on You with a heart filled with faith. I will wait on You with an expectant heart. And even as I wait on You, Lord, I hold on to Your promise in Isaiah 40:31 (NKJV) which says: But those who wait on the Lord shall renew their strength; they shall mount up with wings like eagles, they shall run and not be weary, they shall walk and not faint.

As I pray, Lord, develop patience within me. Renew my strength, Father. Let me not be distracted, discouraged or dismayed, as I wait patiently on You.

You know my needs. You know my requests before I can even utter a word. I trust You and know You to be a God who is faithful to provide for me and meet me at my point of need.

I bless Your holy name, King Jesus. I thank You for the privilege of being able to come before You in prayer. You are great and mighty, and I will be still and know that You are God.

Thank You for hearing my prayer,

Amen and amen.

THE POWER OF GOD'S WORD

When problems arise and we find our backs against the wall, the Word of God has to be a source of encouragement to us. The Word of God has to be that which ignites the fire in our faith. It reinvigorates our hope and belief so that, regardless of what you're facing, despite the size of the enemy, despite whatever is taking place in our lives, we have a divine and heavenly insurance policy which is the Word of God.

Now I urge you to look at Luke, chapter 4 closely. Jesus was in the wilderness and He was tempted by the devil.

Luke 4:3-4 (NKJV) says: [3] And the devil said to Him, "If You are the Son of God, command this stone to become bread." [4] But Jesus answered him, saying, "It is written, 'Man shall not live by bread alone, but by every word of God.'"

In verses 5 to 7, the devil continues his advances and offers Jesus the kingdoms of the world. But in Luke 4:8 (NKJV), here's Jesus' response: And Jesus answered and said to him, "Get behind Me, Satan! For it is written, 'You shall worship the Lord your God, and Him only you shall serve.'"

Now the devil was audacious, and he thought to try and tempt Jesus a third time. In verse 9, he takes Jesus to Jerusalem and has Him stand on the highest point of the temple, saying, "If You are the Son of God, throw Yourself down from here."

But once again, Jesus responds in Luke 4:12-13 (NKJV) saying: [12] And Jesus answered and said to him, "It has been said, 'You shall not tempt the Lord your God.' " [13] Now when the devil had ended every temptation, he departed from Him until an opportune time.

Now I want you to understand that the devil tempted Jesus three times, and each time Jesus referred to the Word of God. The devil knocked three times, and each time he was answered with the Word of God. The devil offered riches, he said if it's money you want, worship me. If it's power you want, worship me. Jesus was offered the kingdoms of this world by Satan, but Jesus was content. He was full of God's Word. He was satisfied with God's Word. Three times Jesus responded by saying "It is written", and He referred to the Word of God.

Now let me ask you, people of God, when the devil tempts you, how will you respond? What will you say? When the devil knocks on the door of your house, and tries to convince you to let him in, how will you respond? Do you have enough of God's Word in you to resist? Do you have enough of God's Word in you to fight?

We need to dwell and meditate on the Word of God, because it tells us all we need to know about how to resist the devil, how to defeat the devil, and how to be protected against the devil.

1 Peter 5:8-10 (NKJV) says, "8 Be sober, be vigilant; because your adversary the devil walks about like a roaring lion, seeking whom he may devour. 9 Resist him, steadfast in the faith, knowing that the same sufferings are experienced by your brotherhood in the world. 10 But may the God of all grace, who called us to His eternal glory by Christ Jesus, after you have suffered a while, perfect, establish, strengthen, and settle *you*."

PRAYER

Lord Jesus,

You are great and mighty. I pray that Your Word may be kept hidden in my heart. May I live my life according to the principles and commands that are in Your Word. I pray that the Holy Spirit will bring the Word of God to life for me. May Your Word be engrained in my heart.

God, should the devil try to tempt me, let Your Word rise up within me and strengthen me. Should the devil try to lure me with riches, fame or anything in this world, help me to hold on to Your Word. Help me to remember that Your Word, in 1 Corinthians 10:13 (NKJV) says, "No temptation has overtaken you except such as is common to man; but God is faithful, who will not allow you to be tempted beyond what you are able, but with the temptation will also make the way of escape, that you may be able to bear it."

Lord it's in You that I find satisfaction, it's in You that I find contentment. If I hunger, You are the bread of life. If I thirst, I will come to You, Jesus, because I know that in You, my heart will overflow with rivers of living water.

Keep me strong, Lord Jesus. Help me to reject the advances of Satan. Help me to declare Your Word when I am confronted by evil.

I stand on Your Word that says, in Isaiah 41:13 (ESV), "For I, the Lord your God, hold your right hand; it is I who say to you, 'Fear not, I am the one who helps you.' "

I thank You for such a promise. I will not fear, because my help comes from an Almighty God. Although the devil may work against me, I trust You to help me, Lord. Although my enemies may come against me, I trust You to be my defender, Lord Jesus.

Indeed, a thousand may fall at my side, and ten thousand at my right hand; but it shall not come near me because I have Jesus Christ as my refuge.

Lord, I stand on Your Word that says, in Psalm 27:1 (ESV), "The Lord is my light and my salvation; whom shall I fear? The Lord is the stronghold of my life; of whom shall I be afraid?"

Although the struggles of life may come in all shapes and sizes, You, my Lord, are a stronghold in the day of trouble. I am secured by Your promises, Lord. You are a God who has never lost a battle, a God who has never been defeated nor can ever be defeated! So whatever comes against me, I know that I have a strong and Almighty God fighting for me.

Father, I pray and declare that I have victory in Jesus. I declare that I am more than a conqueror according to God's Word. I am covered by the blood of Jesus Christ.

Be praised, Master, be glorified.

Thank You for hearing my prayer.

In Jesus' name I pray,

Amen.

THE WAY WE BEAT THE DEVIL

Revelation 12:12 (NKJV)
"Therefore rejoice, O heavens, and you who dwell in them!
Woe to the inhabitants of the earth and the sea! For the devil
has come down to you, having great wrath, because he knows
that he has a short time."

Now I want to emphasize the last sentence in this passage of scripture. The bible says "...The devil has come down to you, having great wrath, because he knows that he has a short time."

This is a verse that we need to take seriously. We need to be a people who abide in God's presence, always, because there are eternal consequences when we are outside of God's will.

You see, the devil is always looking for opportunities to lead people away from God and set them on the path of destruction. The enemy schemes tactfully and is described as the father of lies because he aims to bring deception and destruction in our lives. Now because of the onslaught of attacks from the devil, sometimes we may be in a position where we have more questions than answers. But I want to remind you that we have a saviour in Jesus. Life as a Christian means that we will have to fight. We will have to fight on our knees and fight using God's Word but, in the end, you will come to find that we have a saviour in Jesus Christ.

1 John 4:4 (ESV) says: "Little children, you are from God and have overcome them, for he who is in you is greater than he who is in the world."

The way we beat the devil is not through any physical strength or internal motivation. We cannot physically land a blow to the enemy. However, the way we beat the devil is by calling upon the name he cannot stand, the name of Jesus Christ.

Jesus is the light that drives out the darkness. At the name of Jesus, Satan has to flee, demons have to tremble, and nature has to bow down. Christ alone has ultimate authority over all creation, and He has promised to be with us in every struggle.

Sometimes, we can't avoid the rough waters of life. We can't avoid the battles of life. Now, although we may not be able to change our circumstances as quickly as we'd like, we can hold on to the fact that we have a saviour in Jesus Christ. We can hold on to the beautiful and uplifting promises in the Bible. Promises like those found in Isaiah 43:2 (NIV): "When you pass through the waters, I will be with you; and when you pass through the rivers, they shall not sweep over you. When you walk through the fire, you will not be burned; the flames will not set you ablaze."

For any problem, any danger or threat, remember that God is with you. If we can only walk by faith, not by sight, we will see the hand of God moving and protecting us from harm.

After all, God has already declared that no weapon formed against us shall stand and if He is for us, who can be against us?

PRAYER

God Almighty,

You are all powerful and mighty. You are the God who made all things. You alone can speak and create, so I bow down and praise You Master. There is none who can come against You, God, and I trust You with all of my cares. I commit all of my ways to You. I give You all of my burdens.

Lord Jesus, I give You the throne to my heart, and I ask that You take control, Lord. Take control of my life and lead me. Take control of my emotions and my thoughts. I trust in You, Lord. You are my Redeemer and the Lord of hosts. You are the first and the last, the Alpha and Omega.

Your Word in 1 John 5:4-5 (NKJV) says: "4 For whatever is born of God overcomes the world. And this is the victory that has overcome the world - our faith. 5 Who is he who overcomes the world, but he who believes that Jesus is the Son of God?"

Lord, I thank You for making me an overcomer. I thank You, because I am more than a conqueror because of You, Lord Jesus. I thank You, because Your Word tells me that You will make me the head and not the tail. You will put me on top and never on the bottom. Father, I praise You for this Word, because when I am hard pressed on every side, I will remember that Jesus Christ has made me an overcomer. When I am pressed down, Lord, I will remember Your Word that tells me that I can do all things through Christ who strengthens me.

You, King Jesus, have overcome the world. You have overcome death, the devil, and every challenge that I could possibly face. You are triumphant, Lord Jesus. Because of You, the devil is defeated and death has lost its sting.

Holy Spirit, help me to be strong in the Lord and in the power of His might. Help me to put on the whole armour of God, so that I may be able to stand against the wiles of the devil. Holy Spirit, I pray that You will help me to put into practice what the Word of God says in Ephesians 6:14-18 (NKJV):

> *14 Stand therefore, having girded your waist with truth, having put on the breastplate of righteousness, 15 and having shod your feet with the preparation of the gospel of peace; 16 above all, taking the shield of faith with which you will be able to quench all the fiery darts of the wicked one. 17 And take the helmet of salvation, and the sword of the Spirit, which is the word of God; 18 praying always with all prayer and supplication in the Spirit, being watchful*

to this end with all perseverance and supplication for all the saints.

Holy Spirit, help me to take up the whole armour of God, so that when the day of evil comes, I may be able to stand on God's Word, to stand in faith and to stand on the Lord's promises.

Lord Jesus, I praise Your name. You are worthy of all of my adoration. You are the first and the last. You are the King of Kings and the Lord of Lords.

I thank You for hearing my prayer.

In the mighty name of Jesus Christ I pray,

Amen.

NOT ASHAMED OF THE GOSPEL

One of my favourite verses in the Bible is Romans 1:16 (NKJV). It reads, "For I am not ashamed of the gospel of Christ, for it is the power of God to salvation for everyone who believes, for the Jew first and also for the Greek."

Pay attention to those words: "...I am not ashamed of the gospel of Christ..."

A lot of people in this world have things that they are proud of and, equally, a lot of people have things that they are ashamed of. Now when it comes to us, as children of God, are we ashamed of the gospel of Jesus Christ? Are we ashamed to say that, "I am a Christian who believes in the death, burial, and the resurrection of Jesus Christ?" Are we ashamed to say that, "I am a Christian who believes that one day the Lord Himself will descend from heaven with a shout, with the voice of an archangel, and with the trumpet of God. And the dead in Christ will rise first. Then we who are alive and remain shall be caught up together with them in the clouds to meet the Lord in the air. And thus we shall always be with the Lord (1 Thessalonians 4:16-17). Are we ashamed to tell our co-workers things like, "I believe that heaven is a real place, hell is a real place, and if you reject Jesus Christ, you will spend eternity in hell. But if you accept Jesus Christ, as Your Lord and Saviour, then you will enter eternal life."

Are we ashamed of the gospel of Jesus Christ? Are we ashamed to tell our friends and family that we all need to turn towards Jesus Christ and repent, for the Kingdom of God is at hand?

As believers, we should not be ashamed of the gospel of Jesus Christ! We should not be ashamed of the gospel, because the devil and the world are aggressively spreading a message of deception. The devil in this world is aggressively trying to lead people away from the saving gospel of Jesus Christ.

However, it is time that we, as believers of Jesus Christ, stand up and declare to the world that there is a Saviour. There is someone who can set you free if you're bound, there is a Redeemer and His name is Jesus Christ. Saints, we should not be ashamed of the gospel, but as Christians, we must stand up and fight to declare the gospel. We must rise up, as sons and daughters of the most high, and proclaim that Jesus Christ is Lord! We must proclaim, "For I am not ashamed of the gospel of Christ, for it is the power of God to salvation for everyone who believes."

I encourage you to be bold. As the voice of the world gets louder, the voice of the church must also become louder. Our voices, as believers, must also be louder, and we must tell every soul we can that Jesus is Lord and Jesus is King!

I encourage you not be silent. Refuse to be silenced by the world. Tell them of Jesus. Speak of Jesus. Shout about Jesus! And do not be ashamed of the gospel.

PRAYER

Lord Jesus,

I praise You, and I honour You. I exalt Your name, Lord.

I pray that I will be filled with the Holy Spirit, and empowered by the Holy Spirit, so that I can boldly declare the gospel of Jesus Christ to all who will listen.

King Jesus, fill me with courage. Fill me with the courage to stand and testify of Your goodness and Your mercy. You, Lord Jesus, have lifted me up out of a pit of despair and You have set my feet on solid ground and given me a firm place to stand. For that I praise You.

Lord, Your Word in Acts 1:8 (NKJV) says, "But you shall receive power when the Holy Spirit has come upon you; and you shall be witnesses to Me in Jerusalem, and in all Judea and Samaria, and to the end of the earth."

Lord, I believe that the Holy Ghost is my helper. I pray that He may help me to grow in wisdom and understanding when it comes to all things concerning the kingdom of God. Holy Spirit, reveal to me the deep and hidden things that are in the Word of God. Fill me with boldness and courage in my walk with Christ.

Empower me to tell all who will listen about the true gospel of Jesus Christ. Holy Spirit, help me to testify about the goodness of God and all that he has done for me. Make me a strong Christian who is unashamed of the gospel of Christ.

Father, I pray that you would help me to realize my role within the body of Christ. If I am called to be a missionary, Holy Spirit, empower me to preach the gospel of Christ. If I am called to support those who are preaching the gospel, Holy Spirit, empower me to do all I can to support the advancing of the gospel into the world. If I am called to sing and worship, empower me, Holy Spirit, to sing and bring glory to the name of Jesus Christ. Holy Spirit, empower me and give me the courage to use my gifts, my talents, my abilities, all so that I can give glory to God!

Lord, Your Word in Mark 16:15 (NKJV) says, "And He said to them, 'Go into all the world and preach the gospel to every creature.'"

Dear Father, in this world that is filled with sin, I pray that you would raise me up to be among those believers who are unashamed to preach the gospel of Jesus Christ. Let me not be afraid or timid when it comes to declaring Your Word, Lord Jesus.

I pray that Your light will shine in my life and through my life. I pray that others may see how You have turned my life around, and may my life point others to Jesus Christ. God, I pray that You will give me wisdom when I speak to people. Let my words point to Jesus

Christ as the answer to all things. Let my actions bear witness to the saving grace of Jesus Christ.

Lord, should the forces of evil arise to try and discourage me or intimidate me to remain silent, let Your power fall and break every plan and device from the enemy. Be my sun and my shield, Lord. I humble myself before You and declare that I cannot go through this life without You. I need You, Lord Jesus.

I pray that You will deliver me from every stronghold that seeks to silence me. Strengthen me against every foe, guide me and order my steps, lead me through every valley, and be with me on every mountain.

Rule and reign in my life, King Jesus.

Be lifted high for evermore,

Amen.

LET GO OF EVERYTHING WEIGHING YOU DOWN

Hebrews 12:1 (NKJV)
"Therefore we also, since we are surrounded by so great a cloud of witnesses, let us lay aside every weight, and the sin which so easily ensnares us, and let us run with endurance the race that is set before us."

Now, I would like to pay particular attention to the phrase, "...let us lay aside every weight, and the sin which so easily ensnares us..."

Looking at various translations for this verse, the Bible here is telling us to throw off everything that hinders us, and to let go of every sin that so easily entangles us. It's telling us to strip off every weight that slows us down, especially the sin that so easily trips us up.

All in all, you and I need to stop for a moment and look at our lives. What weight are you carrying around? What's the thing that has you bound and pressed down? Because, in order for us to progress in this race of faith, we need to get rid, we need to lay aside, we need to throw off and strip off anything and everything that is pulling us backwards.

In life, friends can become a type of weight that slows you down. Your friends, the company you keep, can become hindrance in your walk with God and in other areas of life. What you feed and dwell on can become a weight and a hindrance if you're not careful. The novels you spend hours reading, those movies or TV shows you binge watch, that music that you listen to all day, all of these things could really be pulling you back as a child of God.

Or how about money? The pursuit of money, and especially the love of money, can be a hindrance to how far you will progress in this race of faith. All of these things can trip us up as we run towards Jesus. And this is an important message, because a lot of people are unknowingly tripping themselves up in their walk with God because of what they entertain. A lot of people are carrying around unnecessary weight that is hindering them, when they could be enjoying a deeper fellowship with the Lord.

On this topic, I love the directness of Matthew 18:8-9 (NKJV), because the Bible says, "8 If your hand or foot causes you to sin, cut it off and cast it from you. It is better for you to enter into life lame or maimed, rather than having two hands or two feet, to be cast into the everlasting fire. 9 And if your eye causes you to sin, pluck it out and cast it from you. It is better for you to enter into life with one eye, rather than having two eyes, to be cast into hell fire."

What Jesus is talking about here is exactly what Hebrews 12 : 1 is talking about when it says, "...let us lay aside every weight, and the sin which so easily ensnares us..."

The bottom line is, if it causes you to sin, cut it out. If it's causing you to drift away from God, cut it out. If it's tempting you and luring you to sin, cut it out!

PRAYER

Dear Lord Jesus,

You are the King of Kings. You are the Lord of Lords. I pray that I will be filled with the Holy Spirit to such an extent that my eyes will be opened. Open my eyes to see all that is pulling me back. Open my eyes so I can see everything that is hurting my walk with You. Help me to see who or what I have allowed in my life that should not be there.

Lord, I surrender to You, and I give You permission to do as You please in my life. If I have people around me who are pulling me back and discouraging me, remove me from such company. If I am pursuing wealth, money and riches, instead of seeking You first, I pray that You will remove this desire from me.

Your Word commands me to repent and turn away from sin. Help me to be obedient to this command Lord.

Have mercy on me, Lord, and help me to identify that which is causing me to sin in my life. Give me the strength to cut it out. Give me the strength to walk away.

Father, for every desire that does not glorify You, I pray that You will remove it from my heart. For every plan that doesn't involve You, or any plan that seeks to feed my selfish ambition, remove it from me, Lord.

Your Word in Job 11:14 (ESV) says, "If iniquity is in your hand, put it far away, and let not injustice dwell in your tents."

Lord, if sin is in my life, help me to put it far away from me. Let there be no wrongdoing in my life.

I pray and declare Psalm 51:1-2 (NKJV) which says, "[1] Have mercy upon me, O God, according to Your lovingkindness; According to the multitude of Your tender mercies, blot out my transgressions. [2] Wash me thoroughly from my iniquity, and cleanse me from my sin."

Lord I thank You for Your loving-kindness. I thank You for Your tender mercies. As I strive to walk in obedience to Your Word, I pray that You will strengthen me and give me the grace to stand strong and resist temptation. Give me the strength to resist the devil. My desire, Lord, is to run the good race of faith.

Your Word in Hebrews 12:1-2 (NKJV) says, "[1] Therefore we also, since we are surrounded by so great a cloud of witnesses, let us lay aside every weight, and the sin which so easily ensnares us, and let us run with endurance the race that is set before us, [2] looking unto Jesus, the author and finisher of our faith, who for the joy that was set before Him endured the cross, despising the shame, and has sat down at the right hand of the throne of God."

Lord, I pray that the Holy Spirit will help me to strip off every unnecessary weight that works to hinder me in my walk with You. Instead, I pray that my eyes will forever be looking unto Jesus, the author and finisher of my faith.

Be glorified, my God.

In Jesus' name I pray,

Amen.

YOUR WORDS AND YOUR HEART

Have you ever thought about how close a connection there is between your words and what's going on in your heart?

Yes... what we say reveals what's in our hearts. The words that we speak reveal the contents of our hearts. You can pick up if someone is genuinely filled by the Word of God by the contents of their speech. You cannot meditate and dwell on God's Word but then fail to talk about it. His Word will be reflected in your speech if it's really rooted in your heart. However, for a heart filled with sin and evil, you will find that the corruption and worldliness in that heart will be reflected in that person's speech.

Luke 6:45 (ESV) says, "The good person out of the good treasure of his heart produces good, and the evil person out of his evil treasure produces evil, for out of the abundance of the heart his mouth speaks."

The Amplified Bible translation for this same verse says, "The [intrinsically] good man produces what is good and honourable and moral out of the good treasure [stored] in his heart; and the [intrinsically] evil man produces what is wicked and depraved out of the evil [in his heart]; for his mouth speaks from the overflow of his heart."

In our own lives, we have to be asking the question, what are some of the things that are coming out of my mouth? What have you stored in your heart, because out of the abundance of the heart, the mouth speaks. So if God's Word is what's stored in your heart then, inevitably, your words will reflect that.

Have you ever wondered why and how people can recite the lyrics to a song that came out years ago, but they can't recite more than three Bible verses? It's all to do with what's in the heart and what they decide to dwell on. We should be mindful about what we are feeding on, what we are dwelling and meditating on. What are you consuming? Is it the Word of God, or is it worldly entertainment? Because that will be reflected when you speak.

Now not only are words a reflection of what's in your heart, but words have power. The Bible says in Proverbs 18:21 (KJV), "Death and life are in the power of the tongue: and they that love it shall eat the fruit thereof." Meaning our tongues can either build or tear down. Our tongues can curse or bless. They can declare the Word of God and speak life into a situation, or they can speak destruction.

Think about that and consider, how are your words affecting you? How are they shaping your life? How are they impacting your future?

Now with that said, Proverbs 15:4 (NKJV) says, "A wholesome tongue is a tree of life, but perverseness in it breaks the spirit."

The Bible likens a wholesome tongue, a clean, virtuous and pure tongue to a tree of life. Your words have power and they have even more power when you combine them with faith and the Word of God.

I encourage you to pray for wisdom and grace when it comes to the words that you speak. May they be words that are always pleasing to the Lord. Our prayer ought to be that our lips will always be full of praises to the Lord. The words we speak ought to encourage others in the faith, they ought to testify about the goodness of Jesus Christ and they should never destroy another believer's faith.

PRAYER

King Jesus,

You are an awesome and mighty God. I praise You for Your amazing grace and love. Father, my prayer is that you will transform my heart so that the words I speak will be wholesome and acceptable to you. I pray that my words will build and encourage those around me. Give me a wholesome tongue, Lord, so that I may be found to be speaking words that impact my life in a positive and Godly way. I pray that You will give me a wholesome tongue so that I may speak words that are in line with Your will and purpose for me.

Change my heart so that the words that come out of my mouth will be a reflection of Your transformative work. Change my heart, King Jesus, so that my words will be words of faith, hope, and victory. Holy Spirit, I pray that You will guide me and give me the presence of mind to always speak positive words of faith and victory. Let there be no corrupt words that come out of my mouth.

Lord, I pray that I will not use my words to simply describe the situation I find myself in but, through the authority that's in the name of Jesus Christ, I will speak God's Word into my situation and into my circumstances. I will speak God's Word and believe that, in the end, Father, Your will is what will be done.

Holy Spirit, help me so that I may not have a tongue that always speaks about how big my problems are, but give me a tongue that always testifies about how mighty and awesome my God is.

Father, Your Word in Proverbs 6:2 (NKJV) tells me that, "You are snared by the words of your mouth; You are taken by the words of your mouth." Therefore, I choose to declare your goodness over my life. I declare that I am expecting my God to overwhelm me with His goodness and love. I stand and declare Psalm 31:19 (NKJV) which says, "Oh, how great is Your goodness, which You have laid up for those who fear You, which You have prepared for those who trust in You in the presence of the sons of men!"

I pray that I will continue to experience Your hand over my life, Lord Jesus. I pray that my family and I will continue to experience Your kindness and faithfulness in a mighty way. Your love, Lord, and Your amazing grace means that I will not be discouraged by anything that life brings my way. Because of You, Lord, I will not worry. I will not doubt. I will not fear, but instead I will keep my trust in You, knowing that You are a God who never fails. You are a God who will never let me down.

Your Word says in Luke 21:15 (ESV), "For I will give you a mouth and wisdom, which none of your adversaries will be able to withstand or contradict."

I receive this promise, Father. Give me a mouth filled with wisdom, a mouth that is aware of the power and significance of my words. I pray that out of the abundance of my heart, I may speak Your Word, Lord. May I speak about Your love and Your amazing grace, and the unmerited favour that is upon my life and my home.

Be blessed and glorified. In Jesus' name,

Amen.

KNOWING WHO GOD IS

Who is God?

What a question, right?

Well, to answer this question, we need to start by looking in the Word of God. What does the Word of God say about who God is?

1 John 4: 8 (NKJV) says, "He who does not love does not know God, for God is love."

1 Corinthians 10:13 (NKJV) says, "No temptation has overtaken you except such as is common to man; but God is faithful, who will not allow you to be tempted beyond what you are able, but with the temptation will also make the way of escape, that you may be able to bear it."

1 John 1:5 (NKJV) says, "This is the message which we have heard from Him and declare to you, that God is light and in Him is no darkness at all."

Numbers 23:19 (NKJV) says, "God is not a man, that He should lie, Nor a son of man, that He should repent.

Has He said, and will He not do? Or has He spoken, and will He not make it good?"

Psalm 116:5 (NKJV) says, "Gracious is the Lord, and righteous; Yes, our God is merciful."

And finally, Psalm 84:11 (NKJV), "For the Lord God is a sun and shield; The Lord will give grace and glory; No good thing will He withhold From those who walk uprightly."

So from these few passages of scripture, we can learn the following: God is love, God is faithful, God is light and in Him there is no darkness at all. God is not a man that He should lie. God is a sun and shield, and God is merciful.

We serve a living God, an awesome and all-powerful God, a God who reveals himself in His Word. He is revealed in scripture. John 1:1 (NIV) says, "In the beginning was the Word, and the Word was with God, and the Word was God." So, for anyone who can't answer the question "Who is God?", the first thing I will tell you is that you can find God in His Word. This is why it's so important for us to spend time meditating on His Word, so that we may know Him.

John 1:14 (NKJV) says, "And the Word became flesh and dwelt among us, and we beheld His glory, the glory as of the only begotten of the Father, full of grace and truth." The Word became flesh when Jesus Christ was born of a virgin so that we could be saved from the punishment of our sins. This is why you and I need to receive Jesus Christ as our Lord and Saviour, because Jesus Christ is the way, and the truth, and the life, and no one comes to the Father except through Him.

One thing I find encouraging about the Bible is that it speaks about God in the present tense. God is full of compassion. God is light. God is love. God is merciful.

Over and over again, the Bible says God is... And we should be strengthened by this; strengthened by the fact that our God is living.

We need to praise and acknowledge God for who He truly is. He is love. He is mercy. He is light. God is 'the Great I Am.' God is almighty!

We must respect His Word, and we must revere Him for His glorious work. We must adore Him for being so powerful but yet so tender and caring to us.

PRAYER

My heavenly Father, the one who holds all of creation in His hands.

I thank You for Your goodness. I thank You for loving me, sustaining me and giving me life. I thank You for caring so much that You gave Your only begotten son, Jesus Christ, so that I may live and not perish, so that I may not be destroyed but so that I may be saved.

Thank You, Almighty God, for Your precious son, the precious Lamb of God, Jesus Christ. My saviour was crucified on a cross for me so that, today, I can say that I am redeemed, I am loved, and I am set free by the blood of Jesus Christ.

Lord, You deserve all glory; all the glory for Your awesome power.

Just as the book of Isaiah 40:14 (NIV) says, "Whom did the Lord consult to enlighten him, and who taught him the right way? Who was it that taught him knowledge, or showed him the path of understanding?" There is no one who can enlighten You, because You are all knowing and You are the God of light. There is nothing that anyone can teach You, because You are filled with infinite wisdom. Your ways are higher than ours. Your thoughts are higher than our thoughts. You are a God of great power, might, and strength.

Father, I thank You for being faithful, because if You turned Your back on me where would I be? Without Your love and mercy God, where would I be? Without the precious sacrifice of Your son, Jesus Christ... God, where would I be?

I am here because of You, and I praise You and worship You. Your Word says that You are enthroned above the circle of the earth, and people are as powerless as grasshoppers before You. Angels surround Your glorious throne and sing "holy, holy, holy to the Lord God Almighty."

There are no words to properly describe Your awesome nature, Your infinite wisdom, and Your supernatural power. So, today, I offer up my praises to You. There is nothing else that I can give You but my heart, my praise, and my adoration. You are my unfailing protector who gives me an eternal home. You are a God who watches over me and my family, and I praise You for You have never let me down.

There is no one else like You, Father. The Bible in 1 Timothy 2:5 (NKJV) says, "For there is one God and one Mediator between God and men, the Man Christ Jesus."

Lord Jesus, I thank You for being my rock and pillar. Thank You for being my saviour and rescue. I will rejoice always, and I will give You my thanks in all circumstances, because You have a plan for my life that is divine and for a greater purpose. I trust that all of my steps are ordered by You. I have confidence in Your Word that tells me to approach the throne of grace boldly, and that if I ask anything according to Your will, then I know that You will hear me.

Lord Jesus, thank You for being good to me. Thank You for being patient with me.

Your Word says in Psalms 4:1 (NIV), "Answer me when I call to you, my righteous God. Give me relief from my distress; have mercy on me and hear my prayer."

I trust and believe in You, King Jesus, that You will answer me when I call out Your name. You offer me relief from distress. You offer wholeness from loneliness or insecurities. You offer me love and acceptance when the world would choose to condemn me, and for that I am thankful and I rejoice.

King Jesus, in Your Word, You say that you came that I may have life and have it abundantly. I thank You for dying on the cross for me to set me free from my sins. Thank You for Your sacrifice so that I may be with You in all of eternity.

I pray that my relationship with You will continue to be strengthened day by day. May it continue to grow, and be closer, and more intimate. Be glorified, King Jesus. May You be glorified always.

Thank You for hearing this prayer.

In Jesus' name I pray,

Amen.

SET YOUR MIND ON
THINGS ABOVE

Have you ever taken time out to examine your thought life? Because each and every one of us has a thought life; a pattern of thinking, a way of thinking. When you wake up, you're thinking about something. When you're cooking, you're most likely thinking too. When you're talking to someone, chances are you're thinking about how to respond; perhaps you're thinking that you need to wrap up this conversation, or you may even be thinking about something completely irrelevant to the conversation you're having.

The point that I'm trying to illustrate is that, as humans, we do a lot of thinking. We're always thinking. Thinking of the future, thinking of the past, thinking of the perfect scenario, or thinking about the worst possible outcome.

However today, I would like to encourage you to take your thought life very seriously. The Bible says in Proverbs 23:7 (NKJV), For as he thinks in his heart, so is he. "Eat and drink!" he says to you, But his heart is not with you.

As you think in your heart, so are you. A lot of people are victims of their own thoughts. They are victims of their own thought patterns, and sometimes it's not that God won't work in our lives or move and break down doors in our lives, but rather it's the fact that we lack faith. When you lack faith and allow doubt to fester in your mind and in your heart, this in turn, creates these negative and often destructive ways of thinking.

Now the Bible in Colossians 3:2 (NKJV) says, "Set your mind on things above, not on things on the earth."

I find it compelling that the Bible says "set your mind." We're being told to "put our minds" in a place where we dwell on heavenly things. We're being told to "position our minds" to dwell on heavenly things.

When you set your mind on things above, you begin to establish a Godly pattern of thinking. So ask yourself, why do I think the way I do? Do my thoughts line up with the Word of God? Do you pay attention to what you're thinking, the kind of thoughts that you dwell on, and the things that influence your thinking?

2 Corinthians 10:3-6 (NKJV):

> [3] *For though we walk in the flesh, we do not war according to the flesh.* [4] *For the weapons of our warfare are not carnal but mighty in God for pulling down strongholds,* [5] *casting down arguments and every high thing that exalts itself against the knowledge of God, bringing every thought into*

captivity to the obedience of Christ, [6] and being ready to punish all disobedience when your obedience is fulfilled.

Verse 5 says "...bringing every thought into captivity to the obedience of Christ..." This means every thought in your life should be restrained. It should be bound under the rulership of Jesus Christ.

The battleground is the mind, and we need to be diligent when it comes to what goes on between our ears.

PRAYER

Lord Jesus,

Your Word tells me that I should bring "every thought into captivity to the obedience of Christ."

Lord, I pray that you will help me in this aspect of my life. Help me to guard my thought life. Every sinful thought, Lord, help me to bring it into captivity. For every impure thought, for every selfish thought, Lord, I pray that you will help me to restrain these thoughts and to cast them down.

May the Holy Spirit help me to set my mind on things above. Help me, Holy Ghost, to guard my mind so that I can focus on whatever is true, whatever is honourable, whatever is just, whatever is pure, whatever is lovely, whatever is commendable.

Lord, I pray that my thoughts will be dominated by the Word of God. May my thoughts be dominated by heavenly things. Lord, destroy my old patterns of thinking and transform my mind. Help me to cast down every negative thought. Help me to cast down thoughts of defeat and thoughts that discourage. Holy Spirit let my mind be fixed on what God's Word says about me. May I know that my identity is in Christ. May I know that my strength is drawn from Christ.

Your Word in Romans 12:2 (ESV) says, "Do not be conformed to this world, but be transformed by the renewal of your mind, that by testing you may discern what is the will of God, what is good and acceptable and perfect."

Transform my mind, Lord. Renew my mind. Clear out everything toxic in my thinking. Help me to stop dwelling on the negative. Father, help me not to be defeated in my thinking. "Let the words of my mouth and the meditation of my heart be acceptable in your sight, O Lord," (Psalm 19:14, NKJV).

Lord, Your Word says in Joshua 1:8 (NKJV), "This Book of the Law shall not depart from your mouth, but you shall meditate in it day and night, that you may observe to do according to all that is written in it. For then you will make your way prosperous, and then you will have good success."

Father, give me the grace to meditate on Your Word day and night. I pray that Your Word will not depart from my mouth but instead may it be engrained in my mind. Let my mind be filled with thoughts of faith, thoughts of victory, and thoughts of hope.

James 1:6-8 (NKJV) says, "⁶ But let him ask in faith, with no doubting, for he who doubts is like a wave of the sea driven and tossed by the wind. ⁷ For let not that man suppose that he will receive anything from the Lord; ⁸ he is a double-minded man, unstable in all his ways."

Father, help me not to be double minded. Let there not be a cloud of confusion in my thinking. Remove all doubts from my mind. Let me not be someone who is tossed around by the winds of life, but instead I pray that 1 will be steadfast in faith, strong in faith, and anchored in Your Word.

Be praised, Lord Jesus. 1 trust you for the victory in every area of my life, especially in my mind.

Be exalted and be lifted high Master.

I thank you for listening to my prayer.

In the name of Jesus Christ I pray,

Amen.

GOD IS GOOD ALL THE TIME

Growing up, there was a statement that I heard a lot in church and among churchgoers. That saying was, "God is good all the time, and all the time, God is good."

Now I heard this saying so often that it almost lost its meaning to me at one point. However, this is a powerful declaration that we really need to believe, because we absolutely need to acknowledge and appreciate the goodness of God.

God is good, and He is good all of the time! Psalm 145:8-11 (NKJV) says,

> *"8 The Lord is gracious and full of compassion, Slow to anger and great in mercy.*
> *9 The Lord is good to all, And His tender mercies are over all His works.*
> *10 All Your works shall praise You, O Lord, And Your saints shall bless You.*
> *11 They shall speak of the glory of Your kingdom, And talk of Your power."*

Note these attributes of God. God is gracious. God is full of compassion. God is slow to anger, and God has great mercy, so how can we not say that God is good all the time? Come rain or sunshine, the Lord is good. Whether I have all the silver and gold the world has to offer, or I don't know where my next meal will come from, God doesn't change... He is still a good God!

If my prayer is answered with a yes, or if the answer is a "not yet", God is still good.

1 Chronicles 29:11 (AMP) says, "Yours, O Lord, is the greatness and the power and the glory and the victory and the majesty, indeed everything that is in the heavens and on the earth; Yours is the dominion and kingdom, O Lord, and You exalt Yourself as head over all."

Your circumstances aren't a factor for whether God is good or not, He is worthy to be praised regardless. Too often, we make the mistake of placing God on the same level as people. When it comes to people, we often associate how nice someone is or how good someone is based on what they do for us. However, this is not how God operates. God can answer you with a "no" because He loves you and that "no" will be because He's protecting you. You could be praying for what you think you need, but that request is the very thing that the Lord is protecting you from because, in the long run, that door, that relationship, that car will do more harm than good in your life. So we can never place God at the same level as people. We can never place God at the same level as our circumstances.

All of us, as believers, must acknowledge God for who He truly is, the Almighty! We must respect His

Word, we must revere Him for His glorious work, and we must adore Him for being so powerful but yet so tender and caring to us.

PRAYER

God Almighty,

You are wonderful and worthy of praise.

You are all knowing and all powerful. You don't need to be shown anything, because You are all-seeing. You are a God who sees everything. You see that which is done in the dark. You see that which is hidden in our hearts. You see our intentions and our motives. Your ways, my God, are higher. Your ways are greater.

Your Word in Psalm 25:8-10 (ESV) says,

> "*8 Good and upright is the Lord; therefore he instructs sinners in the way. 9 He leads the humble in what is right, and teaches the humble his way. 10 All the paths of the Lord are steadfast love and faithfulness, for those who keep his covenant and his testimonies.*"

You are indeed good and upright, Lord. Your ways are filled with compassion, mercy, and steadfast love.

Lord Jesus, I thank You for giving Your life for me. You gave Your life for me so that I would not perish. Thank You for Your goodness. Thank You for being good to me. You have been good to me when You could have condemned me. You could have cast me away because of my sins. You could have turned me away from Your Kingdom because of my sins. But instead, Lord Jesus, Your Word tells me that, "If we confess our sins, he is faithful and just to forgive us our sins and to cleanse us from all unrighteousness" (1 John 1:9, ESV). I am grateful for such love.

You, Lord Jesus, are so good to me that I am at a loss for words, I cannot repay You. All I can do is simply thank You and praise You.

Heavenly Master, I pray that You will teach me how to do good. Teach me to do that which is good in Your sight. Teach me to do Your will. Teach me to follow Your instructions.

I pray that the Holy Spirit will be my teacher. I yield my heart to Your leadership, Holy Spirit. I surrender to Your guidance.

Help me to see myself through the Word of God. Your Word tells me that I am a chosen people, a royal priesthood, a holy nation, and God's special possession.

Lord, I am holding on to the promise that is in Your Word, because Psalm 31:19-20 (NKJV) says: [19] Oh, how great is Your goodness, Which You have laid up for those who fear You, Which You have prepared for those who trust in You In the presence of the sons of men! [20] You shall hide them in the secret place of Your presence From the plots of man; You shall keep them secretly in a pavilion From the strife of tongues.

You have stored up treasures for those that fear You and for those who trust in You, because You are a good God and my heart does safely trust in You. I pray that the Holy Spirit will help me to walk with a Godly fear and to revere Him in all of my ways.

I thank You God for being good to me. I thank You for always being faithful, kind, and merciful.

In the mighty name of Jesus Christ I pray,

Amen and amen.

REMEMBER WHAT GOD HAS DONE FOR YOU

If someone were to ask you, "Who is Jesus Christ to you?" How would you respond? If someone were to ask you the question, "What has your God done for you?" How would you respond?

If you were to ask someone like Lazarus to tell you who Jesus Christ is to him, I imagine that he would say something like, "Jesus Christ is the giver of life. He can speak life into a dead situation. He can speak life and resurrect a dead body."

How about if we asked the woman who is unnamed in the Bible; the woman who was known because of her issue of blood? I imagine that she would begin her testimony by saying, "He healed me! I touched the hem of His garment and He healed me. Jesus Christ is a healer. He made me whole."

Someone like the apostle Paul would, in all likelihood, talk about how great the love of Christ is. So great that even a man who was once so filled with hatred for Christians, a man who used to hunt and persecute Christians, could be forgiven, loved, and given the opportunity to turn his life around.

Ruth would testify about how wonderful God's favour was. Job would speak of God's amazing power of restoration and say, "He can restore all that the enemy has stolen. He can restore even when all hope is lost."

So once again, if I asked you the question, "Who is Jesus Christ to you?" How would you respond?

On a personal level, Jesus Christ is my Lord and Saviour, and He is also my protector. He has protected me from attacks that I never saw coming. He has been so gracious to protect me from people who were determined to see my downfall.

And so, what is your testimony? What has the Lord done for you?

A lot of times, to really appreciate the goodness of God in our lives, we need to look back. We need to look back to where we came from and compare to where we are now. We need to look back and see where God has brought us from. That's where our true testimony lies.

Jesus delivered and set a demon-possessed man free, and here's what the Bible says in Luke 8:38-39 (NKJV): 38 Now the man from whom the demons had departed begged Him that he might be with Him. But Jesus sent him away, saying, 39 "Return to your own house, and tell what great things God has done for you." And he went his way and proclaimed throughout the whole city what great things Jesus had done for him.

Now, why did Jesus encourage the man to go and tell of all the great things God had done for him? Because his testimony would encourage others. His testimony would uplift others.

And so, you should give your testimony at every given opportunity. Not so that you can boast, but so that you can glorify Jesus Christ.

Your testimony will help someone's faith. Your testimony will encourage someone who is going through their own challenges. Your testimony will strengthen someone's belief that God can and God will come through for them.

However, the main thing that your testimony should do is that it should bring glory to Jesus Christ.

PRAYER

Lord Jesus,

You are my Master and Saviour. You are the Alpha and Omega, the King of Kings and Lord of Lords. Lord Jesus, I say that You are great and mighty. You are my deliverer, my Redeemer and the soon coming King.

Lord Jesus, I praise You for being the good shepherd. We praise You for being a bridge over troubled waters. You are a friend who sticks closer than a brother.

Lord, I thank You for all that You have done. I thank You, Lord Jesus, because I am not where I used to be. I thank You Lord Jesus because, by Your grace, I am no longer living in sin but I have the strength to fight for righteousness. I thank You for bringing me into the light from the darkness. Thank You for Your amazing grace. Grace and mercy that gave me sight when I was blind. Grace and mercy that found me when I was lost. I praise You.

Lord Jesus, give me the boldness to declare my testimony to all who will listen. Give me the courage and boldness to declare all that You have done for me to everyone who will listen.

May You receive all of the glory for my life. All that I am, all of my achievements, it's all because of You. All I have, my gifts and my talents, it's all because of You, and I praise Your name, because You are holy and righteous. Words aren't enough to express my thanks and gratitude for all You have done for me.

2 Timothy 1:8-9 (NKJV) says, "[8] Therefore do not be ashamed of the testimony of our Lord, nor of me His prisoner, but share with me in the sufferings for the gospel according to the power of God, [9] who has saved us and called us with a holy calling, not according to our works, but according to His own purpose and grace which was given to us in Christ Jesus before time began."

I will not be ashamed to testify about Your goodness, Lord Jesus. I will not be ashamed to speak of all of the great things You have done in my life. Not only did You deliver me from the clutches of death, not only did You save me from eternal damnation but, Lord Jesus, You have called me to follow You and pick up my cross. You have called me to live a life set apart from the world and so I will forever testify of Your saving grace.

Your Word, in Romans 1:16 (NKJV), says, "For I am not ashamed of the gospel of Christ, for it is the power of God to salvation for everyone who believes, for the Jew first and also for the Greek."

I declare that I am not ashamed of the gospel of Jesus Christ. I will declare all that the Lord has done for me for the rest of my days.

I praise You, Lord Jesus. Be glorified. Thank You for hearing my prayer.

In the mighty and precious name of Jesus Christ I pray,

Amen.

TRUST GOD FOR THE FUTURE

Even with the best intentions, you have no idea what the next few weeks and months have in store for you. You can be the most meticulous planner in the world, but even those who plan for tomorrow don't know what tomorrow holds.

Proverbs 27:1 (NKJV) quite rightly warns us by saying, "Do not boast about tomorrow, for you do not know what a day may bring forth."

Now I don't know about you, but I have accepted this as fact. I do not know what tomorrow holds. I do not know what the future holds. But here's what I'll do. Today, while I still have time, I will put my trust in Jesus. Today, while I am living, while I am breathing, I will declare Jesus Christ as my Lord and Saviour. Today, while I have strength in my body, while I am of sound mind, I will trust in Jesus Christ!

The reason I do not fear the unknown is because the God I trust is an all-knowing God. He is a God who knows what I will face in the future. I am holding on to what the Bible says in Psalm 16:8-10 (NKJV): 8 I have set the Lord always before me; Because He is at my right hand I shall not be moved. [9] Therefore my heart is glad, and my glory rejoices; My flesh also will rest in hope. [10] For You will not leave my soul in Sheol, Nor will You allow Your Holy One to see corruption.

We all have battles awaiting us in the future. Battles that we know nothing about, but I encourage you to set the Lord always before you. Over the coming weeks, months, and years, you don't know what kind of fiery darts the enemy will aim in your direction, so it's vital that you set the Lord always before you!

Don't be afraid. Do not be troubled. Do not tremble at the thought of what this year holds for you, or next year. Instead, set the Lord before you. Put God first and everything else will fall into place!

I don't know how many different ways I can get this message across to you, but do not fear the future, child of God! Don't be fearful of what could happen, or what might happen, or even what has happened. Set the Lord always before you, because Jesus Christ is the Good Shepherd!

The Lord is working for your good! God cares for you! The Lord is a refuge and a safe place. When you call on the name of Jesus Christ, He will come to your rescue. When the righteous cry out, the Lord hears them; He delivers them from all of their troubles.

So trust in the Lord. Remain focused on the Lord, and set the Lord always before you.

PRAYER

Lord Jesus,

I praise You. I praise You, because You know the unknown. You know my beginning from my end. You are wise in all of Your ways. You are triumphant and mighty.

I declare Your Word, in 1 Corinthians 15:57 (NKJV), which says, "But thanks be to God, who gives us the victory through our Lord Jesus Christ."

I declare Your Word in Romans 8:37 (NKJV), "Yet in all these things we are more than conquerors through Him who loved us."

As a child of the Most High King, I am indeed more than a conqueror through You, Lord Jesus. You loved me enough to die for my sins and because of Your precious sacrifice, I am more than a conqueror. Sin has no hold over me. Death has no sting. In Jesus I am more than a conqueror.

Fear is conquered in Your name, Lord. Anxiety is conquered in Your name, Lord. Restlessness, a troubled heart, and depression are all conquered by you power. The devil is conquered in the mighty name of Jesus Christ.

Lord, You are my strong tower. You are omnipotent and omnipresent. There is nothing too difficult for You. This is why I will set You always before me. I will always keep my eyes on You Lord Jesus, because with You on my side, I will not be shaken and I will not be moved. With You on my side, I will not be overcome by the cares of the world.

Lord, with You as my good shepherd, I shall not want. I shall not be in lack. I will not be lost or abandoned, because You are leading me. My future is in Your hands, Lord. My life is in Your hands, Lord.

I declare Psalm 23:6 (NKJV), "Surely goodness and mercy shall follow me all the days of my life; And I will dwell in the house of the Lord Forever."

Surely Your goodness, Your mercy, and Your unfailing love shall follow me all the days of my life. I am convinced and I declare that Your goodness, and Your mercy, and Your unfailing love will rest upon my home and my family.

Lord, I praise You, for You are wonderful, You are glorious, You are holy and righteous.

Your Word says, "Let everything that has breath praise the Lord. Praise the Lord!" (Psalm 150:6, NKJV), and I will praise you forevermore.

You are a healer. You are a waymaker and I bow before You. I give You thanks and praise for the blessings that have been released over my life. By faith, I give You thanks for all of my victories.

For the battles that await me in the future, I praise You in advance for the victory. For the struggles that await me in the future, I praise You in advance for the strength to overcome. For the attacks that the enemy has plotted against me, I praise You in advance for Your protection. I thank You for defending me.

Whatever awaits me in the future, I will not be afraid or fearful. However, I will trust in You, King Jesus. I will lean not on my own understanding. I will place my faith in a faithful God.

I thank You, Lord, for hearing this prayer.

In the mighty and precious name of Jesus Christ I pray,

Amen.

YOUR TIME ON THIS EARTH

I would like to remind you that time is short. Life is short. We only have a set number of days on this earth.

Now, there is a passage of scripture that puts this into perspective. Ecclesiastes 3:1-8 (ESV) reads:

¹ For everything there is a season,
and a time for every matter under heaven:
² a time to be born, and a time to die;
a time to plant, and a time to pluck up what is planted;
³ a time to kill, and a time to heal;
a time to break down, and a time to build up;
⁴ a time to weep, and a time to laugh;
a time to mourn, and a time to dance;
⁵ a time to cast away stones, and
a time to gather stones together;
a time to embrace, and a time to refrain from embracing;
⁶ a time to seek, and a time to lose;
a time to keep, and a time to cast away;
⁷ a time to tear, and a time to sew;
a time to keep silence, and a time to speak;
⁸ a time to love, and a time to hate;
a time for war, and a time for peace.

There is a time for everything on this earth. Nothing on this side of heaven lasts forever. Good times don't last forever, but the joy of the Lord is your strength when you believe in Jesus Christ. Equally, bad times, tough times don't last forever, because the Word of God has promised us that joy comes in the morning.

So with this in mind, my message is simple. Don't wait until it's too late. Don't wait until there is not enough time. While you're still breathing, while you're still able-bodied, while you still can. Repent! Repent and live for God.

While you still can, pray without ceasing. While you still have time, seek Jesus Christ with all of your energy, with all of your might. While you still can, call on God's amazing power to help you to overcome your sinful struggles. Call on the Holy Ghost to transform your heart and defeat everything that tries to place itself above God in your life. While you still have time, fight the good fight of faith wholeheartedly.

Life is short, eternity lasts forever, and we need to live like it.

The Bible says in Hebrews 12:1 (NIV), "Therefore, since we are surrounded by such a great cloud of witnesses, let us throw off everything that hinders and the sin that so easily entangles. And let us run with perseverance the race marked out for us."

The Bible is calling us to strip off every unnecessary weight in our lives. Do away with the sin which tries to ensnare you and keep you bound.

People of God, Jesus Christ is all that matters. With the time that you have, live with wisdom and make use of today and serve the Lord while you still can. Our days are numbered, and we must live for God. So in everything you do, put God first! In the midst of everything you go through, trust God always.

PRAYER

Lord Jesus, will You teach me to number my days so that I may have a heart of wisdom. Teach me to live with the fear of the Lord ruling in my heart! Help me to live a life that is led by Godly wisdom.

Your Word in Ezekiel 36:27 (NKJV) says, "I will put My Spirit within you and cause you to walk in My statutes, and you will keep My judgments and do them."

God, I receive Your Spirit. I receive the Holy Spirit and, according to Your Word, I believe that You will put Your Spirit within me and cause me to walk in Your statutes.

Holy Spirit, empower me to walk in holiness. Holy Spirit, empower me to walk with the eyes of faith. Empower me to walk in alignment with God's Word. Help me, Holy Spirit, so that I can let go of every sin, every idol, every addiction that weighs me down in my walk with Christ. Help me to let go of bitterness. Help me to forgive and to let go of any anger and resentment. Give me the grace to live with the attitude that says, "For me, to live is Christ and to die is gain," according to Your Word in Philippians 1:21 (NIV). Eternity is just around the corner. Help me to live with wisdom, Father.

God, I don't know the day or the hour that You will call my name to Your throne. However, I pray that when You do call me, Lord, and when I stand before You, may You find me to be a believer who lives in a manner that pleases You.

With the time that I have here on earth, set my heart ablaze for You and Your kingdom. Don't allow me to be lukewarm. I have made a decision to follow You, Lord, and so I pray that You will help me to make the best use of the time I have here on earth, because the days are evil.

There is a battle to do right and wrong every day! A battle to live in sin or holiness. In this relentless battle, help me to never lose sight of You and Your wonderful promises. Help me never to lose sight of what Your Word says in John 14:1-4 (ESV):

"1 Let not your hearts be troubled. Believe in God; believe also in me. 2 In my Father's house are many rooms. If it were not so, would I have told you that I go to prepare a place for you? 3 And if I go and prepare a place for you, I will come again and will take you to myself, that where I am you may be also. 4 And you know the way to where I am going."

Lord, I embrace this promise. As I live this life, Father, I want to be found to be in obedience to You, to Your will, to Your authority, to Your kingdom, and to all Your ways.

I surrender my flesh to the will of Jesus Christ. I do not want to be led or attracted to earthly pleasures. Lord, as Your child, give me the mind of Christ where I pursue godliness each and every day. I want to be rooted in Your Word so that I can stand firm against Satan's schemes.

Lord Jesus, You paid a heavy sacrifice for me on the cross and all thanks and glory be unto You, because I now have victory in this life and it's all because of You.

I don't know what tomorrow will bring but, whatever it brings, Jesus is with me. And in Jesus I have a strong refuge in the day of trouble.

I bless Your holy name, and I thank You for listening to this prayer.

In the matchless name of Jesus Christ I pray,

Amen